Oliver Bee is a freelance technology consultant whose passion for surfing and desire to change things up a little bit led him on the odyssey which became *Wave Expectations*. When he's not away surfing somewhere, he lives near Edinburgh with his three children. This is his first book.

To John

Friendship + conversation
are the keys to happiness + fun.
Best of luck with your book -
remember to write with a smile
as the words flow better

Oliver

To Alex, Evie, Harriet and Jenny for supporting this wild ride and laughing with me all the way.

Oliver Bee

WAVE EXPECTATIONS

A Break from the Routine

AUSTIN MACAULEY PUBLISHERS™

LONDON • CAMBRIDGE • NEW YORK • SHARJAH

A CIP catalogue record for this title is available from the British Library.

ISBN 9781398409897 (Paperback)
ISBN 9781398409903 (ePub e-book)

www.austinmacauley.com

First Published (2021)
Austin Macauley Publishers Ltd
25 Canada Square
Canary Wharf
London
E14 5LQ

To Donna, thank you for your friendship, wit and chat.

To Daniela, Nancee, Barbara and Debbie, thank you for letting me join your gang.

To Samantha, Jeff, Brandon and the rest of the team at FAM, thank you for allowing me to help out, even just a little.

To the staff at Austin Macauley, thank you for taking the punt.

Table of Contents

1. Prologue – Breaking the Routine
Nov 2018

So, it was a typical late November Saturday evening in Scotland – days getting shorter, weather getting colder, surf season pretty much coming to an end and thoughts inevitably turning towards Christmas. I'd been out on my board for a couple of hours earlier and caught some decent waves at Belhaven Beach, just east of Edinburgh, and as Jenny, my girlfriend, was out, I was looking forward to a decidedly non-badass night in, consisting of beer, pizza and a movie I just had to work out I would go for.

The first two were simple – with the nearby supermarket reliably well-stocked with whatever beers could take anyone's fancy and a newly opened branch of Dominos just a phone call away, I'd got both of those bases covered. The third, however, was going to require some careful thought as it could make or break the weekend.

Comedy night? *Meh, not really feeling it.*
Rom-com? *Erm, no, not when I'm in on my own.*
Drama? *Nah, not in a worthy enough frame of mind.*

I know, what better way to finish the season than…
Point Break – and obviously the original…

So, my evening was set up, beer on the go, pizza delivered and movie on. I get about 30 to 40 minutes in – Keanu has had some tuition from Lori, he's had his run-in with War Child (yes, yes, I know, I know, but what can you do, I didn't write the script?) and he's starting to mix it with Swayze's crew. There's some amazing footage of huge waves, some barrels and riders performing some wild tricks, when suddenly I'm distracted by the thought, *Jeez, I would love to be able to do that. Even just once. To know instinctively which waves to pick, when to go for it, when to get up, when to turn and then how to bail and bail safely.* This thought is then swiftly followed up by, *Yeah, but it's never going to happen as you're 48, you live on the east coast of Scotland where the waves are fickle, inconsistent and irregular. Oh and you also work five days a week. So, get over it, enjoy the movie, ride the waves when you can and stop being such an eejit.*

So I carried on in a slightly less positive frame of mind until Jenny came back, when I paused it to chat, as I wasn't sure she would want to watch the last half of a film she had seen before. Having established that hers had been a great evening with friends, some superb food and excellent conversation, as opposed to my more sad-sack-on-my-own evening, she asked if I was going to put the movie back on. To which I replied, "Nah, I don't think so," and I explained that the oomph had gone out of it for me due to the above and so didn't need to watch it to the end.

Her response was pretty much the last thing I expected
Jenny: "You really want to get better at this?"

Me: "Well, yeah, definitely."

J: "How long would it take, if you did it every day?"

Me: "Hmm, I don't know, if was able to get out 4/5 days out of 7, a couple of months, maybe."

J: "So why don't you?"

Me: "What do you mean?"

J: "I mean, why don't you go and do it? What's stopping you?"

Me: "Er, well I've got to go to work every day and pay the bills like everyone else."

J: "Really? You work contracts and can leave when your contract finishes with no issue on either side, plus you've got enough savings to cover your bills for the time you're not working."

Me, with a short pause to consider: "Hmm, you know what, you're right, there is no reason why I shouldn't." Further pause. "And to be honest, if I don't do it now, I never will. My current contract is only until March and it's going to be pretty quiet workwise then. I'm pretty sure I can get somewhere relatively cheap to stay on a longish let between LA and San Diego, and flights won't be problem as there are plenty of airports to fly into round there. Right then, that's it. You're on, I'm going to do it."

Result!

…and so, during the next week, I spoke to my boss, who was – let us call it – somewhat surprised, but he listened to my reasoning, which was, "If I wait 10 years, it will be too late. I would just be an old dude in ill-fitting clothes, chasing a pointless dream falling off a board into the water." To which I imagine he was thinking, *As opposed to now, when you would be just a middle-aged dude in ill-fitting clothes*, chasing a pointless dream and *falling off a board into the water*, but he had the decency to both neither to say it nor show it …

With the work situation sorted, I looked at flights, and got a one-way ticket to San Diego from Edinburgh, and over course of the next few days from a good selection of properties to rent between Encinitas near San Diego to Hermosa Beach up by LA, I found what looked like a gem of a place – two bedrooms, large sun terrace, view to the ocean – in a small town called San Clemente, about an hour south of LA and so there I was, all set…

2. How It All Started
Late 70s

As a kid growing up near Blackpool in the '70s and early '80s, I was always going to be a fan of the sea – be it paddling, wave-dodging or swimming. This despite the now well documented issues they have had with beach and sea water cleanliness, but as I said, this was 40 years ago, when such matters were not regarded all that seriously and if they were, it was usually with snorts of derision and comments of the "well, it never did us any harm" sort. Blackpool and the Fylde coast have long been famed for their miles of sandy beaches and gently sloping shoreline, however as it is located on the Irish Sea, the gap between the UK and Ireland is just too short to allow any significant sea-swell to build and therefore does not enable waves large and powerful enough to be formed, which has meant that surfing is never something which took off.

That said, the coastline has always caught a lot of wind and very changeable wind at that. I remember occasions on the beach when the wind would come at me from the front, the back and then from both sides within the space of 15 minutes – very confusing if you're trying to work out which way to set off on a walk (always into the wind to start, as then it helps blow you back, in case you are wondering) and very frustrating if you're trying to light a fire, or something else more illicit. So wind is a feature of the coast and for that reason there are a lot of breeze-based watersports done there, from sailing, kayaking and sand-yachting through to windsurfing and latterly kite-surfing. As with a lot of kids in the area, I had dabbled with many of these, and of them all, I enjoyed windsurfing most of all, as it was just me, the board and the sail against the wind. I managed to get to a reasonably good standard – not competition level, but good enough to remain upright and shifting along for a good half an hour or so before becoming unbalanced or losing the wind and toppling off. – However, as with a lot of childhood pastimes, as I got older, it fell by the wayside as other interests took over.

As a student in the late '80s and early '90s, I lived in Sunderland and then afterwards whilst working I was based in Whitley Bay, near Newcastle, both right by the sea and both close to what are now considered to be excellent surf breaks, but back then, the idea of choosing to go into the North Sea for anything other than a dare or having lost a bet was considered akin to madness. Were I living there now, I would be able to ride waves from Tynemouth near Newcastle all the way up to the Scottish Border and beyond, a good 70 miles of some of the finest and relatively undiscovered beaches with great breaks in the country. After that I did what many do and followed the roads south to London, seeking, not exactly fame and fortune, but certainly a decent job, some new challenges and wider opportunities.

It was fun in the Big Smoke, but not being a city-boy and with starting a family, the bright lights faded over time moving from appealing and attractive to glaring and oppressive and so I began my gradual move northwards via Nottinghamshire to where I am now, just outside Edinburgh and living again by the sea – something distinctly lacking in both London and the Midlands.

That's not to say that I wasn't aware of it, as during childhood family holidays in Cornwall, I'd seen people lying on boards at Newquay, Perranporth and Gwithian beaches and then cruising to shore on waves with huge smiles of satisfaction.

My brother and I must have been so taken with it that we managed to convince our dad to get us one of these boards so that we could have a go ourselves. It was immense fun. It also didn't involve standing up as this was a purely lying down on your stomach type of travel and back then it was called Body Surfing, nowadays it's known by the much cooler name of Boogie Boarding. It certainly wasn't the sort of surfing that Keanu and Patrick were to show the world 10 or so years later and if I'm honest I don't actually recall seeing anyone 'properly' surfing as I expect we were on the more family-sandcastle-burying-a-willing-relative-in-the-sand type of beaches. If I had seen anyone doing that, I am sure I would have been as spell-bound as a kid can be and desperate to give it a go.

So the boogie boarding was great fun and I expect part of that memory stayed with me over the years and led to the other watersports I got involved in. However I wouldn't go as far as to describe it in the manner commonly used nowadays where we are encouraged to talk about being on an "amazing journey", where I made "a deep and lasting bond with the raw power of the sea", as back then we didn't understand about either deep bonds or journeys and besides I was just a nine year old kid and so I think it was much more of "wooooooh, yeeeeaaaah, look at meeeee!" kind of experience. The other things that I know I remember about it were:

1. You stood in the sea with the water at chest/neck level (depending on how brave/foolish you were feeling) with a five mm thick piece of plywood or a thicker chunk of polystyrene, and when any wave approached, you jumped on and kicked your legs like mad to catch it. From memory it worked a surprisingly large amount of the time – although that could well be as a result of the rose-tinted glasses I currently have on.

2. It was mostly me and my older brother doing it whilst our folks watched from the beach. Now, I could be wrong and doing them a great disservice, but they never really liked being in the water, but they did like scrumpy; which was a usual accompaniment with our picnic and this may have been the greater draw for them and before anyone reaches for the phone to call

Social Services, let us just remember, this was the late 1970s after all, when "health" and "safety" were two separate words, rarely used in conjunction with each other and kids were expected to go and entertain themselves...

3. It was bloody cold – it may have been August and we may have been at the most southerly part of the country and benefited the most from the Gulf Stream, but warm it was not. The sun was probably out, but the wind will have been biting, whipping sand across the beach with it and this was also in the days before there were kids' wetsuits and the options for keeping warm were limited and usually involved trudging back up the beach to a sandpaper-level softness towel and then shivering ourselves dry in the 'shelter' offered by the windbreak (remember those?). That said, my dad did have an upper body wetsuit that I put on once or twice, but as it was several sizes too big and filled with water as soon as I hit the sea, I think the greatest lesson I learnt from its use was how not to drown. The question as to why my dad had an upper body wetsuit, when he never went into the sea remains unanswered to this day.

4. Most of all, though, what I remember very clearly is that I was better than my older brother – and when you're nine, I don't think anything comes close to that. Bragging rights were mine for at least a whole three days!

So, there you have it, that was how I had my introduction to catching and riding waves, perhaps not the surfing that everyone thinks of, but it was at least a version of it. I wouldn't day it was a very Hollywood or even very dramatic introduction, but in a lot of ways, I think it was far better than either of those as it was purely about having fun.

3. Back to the Water
Summer 2009

For this next part, we fast forward a number of years – a lot of years, actually – to 2009. As mentioned earlier, I'd tried out a number of water sports throughout my teenage years before location and other priorities intervened and it wasn't until I had my own family that the opportunity to get Back to the Water came along.

We were on a family holiday (the 'we' in this case being me, my wife and our three children), and this was a Big Trip. We were in America, taking a month or so to see Grand Canyon, Las Vegas, Sequoia and Yosemite National Parks, San Francisco and San Diego, before finishing with five nights just outside LA. To say that we had had *The Best Time Ever!* only merely hints at how much fun we'd had. Alex, Evie and Harriet were still young – eleven, nine and four respectively – and so had never experienced anything like this, from the sizes of canyons, mountains and trees to the sizes of cars, roads, and of course, the food portions. Everything was new, it was exciting and very often jaw dropping.

A particular highlight had been the drive down from San Francisco as our route took us along Highway 1 via Carmel and passed Big Sur as it hugs the coast all the way to Santa Barbara – and when I say 'hugs' I really do mean it, as you could not be closer to the Pacific without actually being in it. It is spectacular and breath-taking in equal measure and when you park up and dare yourself to look over the barriers at the ocean, you don't just see how powerful it is, you can actually hear and feel it, as the swell and waves roll in relentlessly hour after hour, day after day crashing into the jagged rocks and sheer cliffs a couple of hundred or so feet below, sending spray shooting high up the cliff-face and making the seabirds dance and skitter.

Having negotiated the hairpin bends and switchbacks to the bottom of the coast road, we left the ocean and carried on with our holiday further inland. To end our trip, we wanted to have a good few days where we were not in the car quite so much, but we still wanted to do some of the typical touristy things, such as a few days on the beach as this would help us unwind and relax before heading home. To do that we decided that rather than be in LA itself we should stay instead in Santa Monica as it is relatively close to the likes of Universal Studios, but is also on the coast with miles and miles of its own beaches and is also big enough to have plenty of its own character and not be swamped by its bigger neighbour. We stayed at the DoubleTree Hotel, which I really only mention, not for commercial reasons, but solely because the reception staff hand out just the most delicious chocolate cookies when guests check in – and also as it happens when the youngest children smile very sweetly at them every time you hand in your key and/or pick it up again.

Having done the officially planned touristy stuff, including Universal (Jaws still attacks the bus on the studio tour), the pier (the official end of Route 66 – which no longer exists), and some retail therapy, before finally getting to the beach later on in the afternoon on day two.

From the pier and driving along the Pacific Coast Highway (or the PCH as locals refer to it), we'd seen a lot of people a reasonable way out who were surfing good and proper, this amazed and impressed us all, as we had never seen it done before. We had also spotted large numbers of people much closer to shore in the breaking water coasting in on shorter boards, but it didn't really click immediately what it was they were doing and it wasn't until we were on the beach and watched them up closely that I realised they were Boogie Boarding. We watched this for a while, as well as mucked about in the surf, before heading back to the hotel.

Next morning, we got up and drove round to Malibu just to have a look around and to be able to say that we'd visited and before we left, went to the supermarket to get drinks and food. Just in the entrance we passed by what looked like some of the shorter boards and we had one of those moments where we all looked at each other and knew exactly what we were thinking. Five minutes later we were the proud smiling owners of a fluorescent yellow, pink and blue foam boogie board.

After that we headed straight to the main beach at Santa Monica and after some comedy hop/walking across the extremely hot sand, 'Ooh, ooh, ouch, ouch!' (note to self, always have flip flops in the car) we hit the waves. It was fabulous and best of all, it was easy as pie – none of us needed more than a couple of goes to learn the technique and we all caught more waves than we could count. This included Harriet, who despite being only four years old, caught some of the best rides as we managed to get her sitting upright on the board, with one of us holding it steady until a wave came along, released the board and then have two of us swimming into shore with her, sitting very serenely and regal, positively queen-like, along with a ginormous smile on her face. We didn't know it at the time, but looking back, I'm pretty sure that's when we caught the surf-bug…

4. Who's Got It Going?
Summer 2012

So, we'd done boogie boarding, surely we could do more and take on bigger challenge? Well, not exactly, in fact, not at all, truth is that we did nothing else – at least not immediately. Living where we did near Edinburgh, it just didn't occur to us that surfing or boogie boarding would be available close to home and the simple fact is that we never looked for it either – this despite having large, open and accessible beaches close at hand. I think that old devil – fear of the cold, cold water – was just too strong. We just replayed the memories and enjoyed the photos of our day on Santa Monica beach and that might have been that, until that is we went to Cornwall in 2012 for our summer holiday…

We were staying in a holiday cottage in Falmouth, which in my opinion is a real gem of place, located as it is on the southern side of Cornwall. It's a bright, colourful and prosperous town with a busy working port and harbour, plenty of pubs, bars, restaurants and lots of independent shops, which bring to it in an open and free spirit feel to the streets. These latter appear to be prospering very happily alongside the more standard high street shops and add a dash of extra zest and local flavour.

In the run up to the holiday we had thought about the sorts of things we would do whilst we were away – beaches, ice cream, castles, ice cream, walks, swimming, ice cream etc. – and so I was very pleasantly surprised when my tentative suggestion that we have a bash at surfing received a universally positive response. Excellent.

Having made a plan, I now needed to get it actioned and thinking it might take some doing I had a quick trawl of Google and found that actually it was going to be pretty straightforward as the number of companies offering surf tuition was vast – maybe I'd been living under a rock for a few years as I had no idea how big and popular an activity it had become. Narrowing my search down to a couple of companies which specialised in teaching families I plumped for the Cornwall Surfing Academy based at Holywell beach as their tagline "We'll get you up in 45 mins" was pretty hard to ignore, no matter how unlikely it seemed. A quick phone call to them had us booked in for a two-hour session along with a repeat of their assertion that we'd all be up and surfing in well under an hour – now how could I possibly turn that down?

As our holiday approached and our appointment with destiny got closer, the excitement started to build and we fuelled this (and gulped a lot) by watching surf videos on YouTube, including one showing where a guy was filmed riding a 40 ft monster in Portugal, after which Harriet asked me rather plaintively, "It won't be like that, will it Daddy?"

Having reassured that we wouldn't be doing that, but also telling her that it may well be quite difficult but definitely lots of fun as well, she brightened up and asked to see the one where a man posing on his board falls off after he gets overtaken by a dog on another board.

We arrived at the surf school on an overcast day to be met by the team who having checked us in, measured us up for wetsuits and told us to go get changed and come back in 20 minutes or so to get boards and head for the beach. There then followed a good 15/20 minutes of rookie wetsuit rigmarole – putting it on backwards, trying to shove heads through arm holes and way more stretching, leaping and tugging than is good for anyone's dignity. Eventually attired, we were given our boards and we set off in a column for the beach to begin our instruction, starting off with the "Goofy test", which revealed that two of us were Goofy-foot and two were not. Goofy-foot is surfer slang for someone who rides a board with their right foot leading, it's not clear why it is so-called, but it does not seem to be connected to Mickey Mouse's friend. Incidentally, if you ride with your left foot leading (i.e. not Goofy), that's just called "Regular" because it's the most common way to stand on a board.

All surf schools follow a similar approach to teaching the basics, which all begin with the boards flat on the beach in a semi-circle around the instructor, everyone lying on their boards and using arms to paddle through the sand, before practising the pop-up via the three stages (push body up from board, get up onto knees, stand up). After 10/15 mins of practice, it was time to hit the water – it all seemed far too simple.

We trooped out to a point where the water was roughly chest/waist-deep level, laid flat on our boards with toes just hanging over the end and waited for our instructor to say, "Good wave coming. OK. Paddle! Paddle! Paddle!"

Immediately we all started to Paddle! Paddle! Paddle! and then we all fell off, swallowed a good amount of Atlantic and laughed at each other. A lot. Undeterred, we went back out, got ourselves set up and again and Paddled! Paddled! Paddled! Hmm, pretty much the same result. This was repeated for a good 10 or 15 minutes or so before things started to change. Evie and I got to our knees before we fell off, Alex and Harriet both managed to get upright, albeit briefly, before falling off, then Evie caught one for five seconds and Alex got one for 10. We still continued to fall off, but the important thing was that we were catching waves. This was a very good feeling.

A further 20 minutes or so, and we were all to a lesser or greater extent getting up and riding, all accompanied by much whooping, fist bumping and cheering. By the end of the two-hour session, we were all catching most of the waves we went for and getting fully upright. The riding of a wave all the way to the beach was granted a special level of *Woop!* and Harriet, being the smallest and lightest, was able to capitalise on this more than most, as she was able to catch them in about a foot of water and pretty much every time reached the beach.

Walking back to the academy, there was much reliving of our triumphs and disasters – competing for who'd had the longest ride, caught the most waves, had the best wipe-out and swallowed the most seawater, etc. The one thing we were able to agree on though was that that was the most fun we'd ever had in the sea.

Not wanting to let the fun end we had to try it again, so we went twice more in the week, both times we went to Perranporth, where we hired boards and wetsuits from the Ticket to Ride surf shop right by the beach and remarkably, we just picked up from where we left off. We did of course continue to fall off and miss waves, but that just made us more determined to get back on and head back out. On the final occasion, we took a disposable camera with us, both to capture the memories, but also we felt we needed an actual record to show to friends and family back home our newfound talents. Alex had so much fun that he was confident enough to paddle that bit further out, and take up the classic pose of sitting astride the board, legs dangling in the water and shooting the breeze with some of the 'dudes' in the line-up who were waiting for their break. Big respect…

Having headed in for the final time and handed back the wetsuits and boards at the surf shop, the owner – who'd earlier been giving a lesson to some other newbies and had seen us – looked at us all and said, "You guys. Wow, third time huh?

That's impressive." Pause. "You really it got it going out there."

And that was all we needed to hear, it was official, we had become surfers.

Could we have been happier?

I don't think so.

5. A Smoother Ride Than Santa
Dec 2012

In December 2012, we had decided that for a festive change we would forego the annual round of turkey, mince pies, tree decorating and family get-togethers and try doing Christmas abroad. As we'd had a such a great time in 2009, we plumped for a return to America to see what a Stateside Yuletide was like. With the vastness of the country and our limited time, we again chose the South West as our destination, mostly because we wanted to have some sunshine and warmth and also because skiing has never been our thing.

Although we had a decent amount of time on this trip – about three weeks as opposed to four last time – our itinerary was still quite extensive as it encompassed Las Vegas, Grand Canyon (stunning in the snow), Joshua Tree National Park, Death Valley, San Diego and one of the beach cities in southern Orange County called San Juan Capistrano (SJC), where we were staying for the five nights over the Christmas period.

SJC was an excellent place to be based as it enabled us to get to Anaheim for Disneyland (which we visited on Christmas Day in the belief that it would be quiet because surely everyone would be at home celebrating the big day? How wrong could we be? Turns out, Dec 25th is usually the House of Mouse's busiest day – it was mobbed – but hey ho, we got on the rides we wanted to.) It was also close to the Irvine Centre where we watched the Hobbit on IMAX (a very immersive experience) as well as trips up and down the

Pacific Coast Highway (PCH) and up as far as Long Beach in the LA burbs.

We stopped in Newport Beach and took the very cool car ferry over to the boardwalk for ice creams, but were disappointed (although not all that surprised) not to find the Bluth Frozen Banana Stand from Arrested Development.

The more we drove along the PCH, the more we watched the ocean and the more we wanted to get in the water and practice the skills we'd learnt in the summer. So one evening on a cruise back towards SJC we stopped at Surf N Paddle in Laguna Beach and enquired about boards, wetsuits and whether it was safe for novices to go out at this time of year. The guy running the shop was very helpful and said that there was good swell coming in the day after next, which would be fine for Alex and me, but probably not for Evie and Harriet given their age and size.

A couple of days later, the two of us duly turned up, got kitted out and were allotted foamboards that the owner thought appropriate. Mine was quite a bit bigger than the one I had used in the Summer in Cornwall, but I didn't say anything, as after all, he was the expert and this was his turf (or surf…). We hit the beach and taking note of the warning about the few underwater boulders in the immediate vicinity, headed near to where there were a couple of other guys out on the water. When we were stood on the sand, the waves had not seemed all that big and we thought this might not be a great success, however once in the ocean, it was clear we were dealing with a very different level of power in the waves and swell. Straightaway, Alex caught what we thought was a small wave, which actually took him all the way back to the beach and it was as if he'd never been out of the water. It took me a while to get the hang of the larger board and so consequently I didn't catch quite as many waves, but I caught enough to more than fill my quota of woops and high fives and it more than showed that we had both managed to retain the knowledge and basic techniques we had learnt in the summer.

Two hours later, having ridden back to the beach again and then finding out that I was too tired to paddle back out, we decided to call it a day. The Pacific really was a whole different ballgame in terms of power and energy. So, weary, but elated, we headed back up to Surf N Paddle to return our gear and it was only after they'd wished us a cheery "Merry Christmas" as we were leaving the shop that we remembered it was Christmas Eve – both of us doubted that Santa would get rides as smooth as us that night.

6. Starting Again
2014

Despite knowing that we really enjoyed surfing, it was over a year before we tried it again – this time, much closer to home. I had come across the Coast to Coast surf school when they had a pop-up tent in St Andrew's Square in Edinburgh as part of an event to showcase local companies who offered coaching on various outdoor activities.

The C2C team were talking about the surfing, coasteering and stand up paddle boarding (SUP) lessons that they run, as well as having a balance board, which is essentially a small surfboard fixed in the middle to a pivot mechanism, the idea being that you stand on it and try to keep your balance. I had taken a leaflet and done what most of us do with such things and promptly put it in my bag and forgot all about it. At work, a month or so later, I was musing on spring being finally here and what I could do to make the most of the predicted good weather this coming weekend, when it occurred to me that I could get out and have another go at surfing. So I dug out the leaflet – which I was pleased to find was still in the bag – phoned the number on it and booked a board and wetsuit hire for the coming Saturday…

The C2C team do all of the surf coaching at Belhaven Beach, which is about 20 miles east of Edinburgh. I met with Sam and Josh who founded and run the business, picked up my board and wetsuit and headed out over the dunes to the shore. Belhaven Beach is perfect for beginner and intermediate level surfers as it is 100% sand, no rocks at all, and its gentle slope leads to waves which are generally pretty smooth when they come in. It took half an hour or so to relearn the basics of Paddle! Paddle! Paddle! Pop-up, but once done, I was up and away and loving every minute. It was helped by a good spring tide swell, which brought in good sets of waves on a pretty regular basis, so that if you missed one, there would be another along shortly after to try again.

I had a really great two hours on the water and when I returned the board I got such a friendly, "See you next week," from Sam, it occurred to me, "You know what, actually, I really do want to do it again," and so it was just a couple of weeks later that Harriet and I were both back out riding waves like we'd never been away. Over the summer, we went out four or five times more steadily improving our skills and helping each other by sharing where we thought we were going wrong and suggesting what we might do to put things right, right, which was just the best way for us build our confidence and learn new moves and tricks.

In the following October Harriet and I went to Portugal for a long weekend, as its coast is famed for its huge waves – in fact it's where the largest waves in the world are often found due to it being on the Atlantic, which enables the large waves to form, and having an almost perfect gently shelving shoreline which enables the waves to roll in in a consistent manner. We went in the hope that we might get some very late summer warmer weather surfing and we stayed just outside Lisbon in a hotel right on Praia do Guincho, which we found out later is one of the best surfing beaches in the Lisbon area.

The beach was stunning, with very unspoilt, deep golden sand but (unfortunately for us) huge waves that would have mashed us into the seabed. We watched open mouthed as 15 ft breaks rolled in off the Atlantic, which then broke and roiled in the shallows, before being torn along the shoreline in a very powerful rip current. We were obviously disappointed not to get out, but in many respects, it was enough just to marvel at the raw strength and energy of the ocean – whilst at the same tome feeling a little bit relieved that the waves hadn't been a that bit smaller when we might have felt compelled to go out.

The following spring and summer saw us going out more and more and we were joined on occasion by Alex and Evie as well, which completed the set up nicely. We also bought our own wetsuits, which although fine for summer use, it fast became clear that come the colder weather they were far too thin (just 3mm) and they were not going to cut the mustard, so we went out and bought thicker and more durable ones.

At summer's end, Harriet started at high school in Edinburgh, which, although it was quite daunting, she was very eager as they're the only school in the city to have a Surf Club, who meet on Wednesdays after school (until it gets too dark and then starts again in the summer term) and accompanied by teachers head down to Belhaven Beach for coaching by the C2C team. These additional sessions helped bring her skills along enormously and after a few weeks, she was invited to join the junior squad so that she could benefit from further training with the potential to enter competitions in the future.

Once the season had ended, C2C announced they were selling off some of their older boards, so off we went like a couple of kids with free rein in the sweetie shop and picked up a couple of boards, which meant we could now load up the car whenever we wanted and head wherever the waves were going to be – we'd finally become surfers!

Own board, will travel…

7. Taking Flight
2015–2018

Confident now that we could catch waves at our regular beaches – Belhaven and St Andrews – what we had to do now was work on those skills so that they become second nature. As a result of both school surfing club and squad training, Harriet was able to gain a fair edge on this, even entering a number of competitions and placing highly against girls and boys in her age group. Her core skills developed well and she learnt plenty of new tricks, turns and moves every time she went out – many of which she tried to pass on to me.

The last couple of summers saw us back out in Southern California, where we stayed in the beach cities of San Clemente and Oceanside. Both places have miles and miles of accessible sandy beaches, with good consistent waves and consequently very active surf scenes.

In July and August, they each play host to ocean festivals, which attract some of the best surfers in the state and consequently, skill levels are extremely high and competition is very tight. Our visit in July 2018 coincided with the build up to the Oceanside festival when a really good swell came in which provided the competitors with plenty of opportunity to practice ahead of the big weekend competitions.

Ahead of our holiday I had got in touch with Eric Alden who is the owner of a long-established surf shop in Oceanside called Up Sports to enquire about the hire of a couple of boards for the duration of our holiday. Ordinarily a board costs about $30-$40 per day to hire and they can be of varying quality and so would mean us shelling out 900 bucks or so for the fortnight for boards which may or may not be any good.

As this was not going to work for us, Eric suggested he buy a couple of brand new boards and sell them to me at cost ($225 each) and if we didn't want to take them home with us, he would buy them back at the end of the holiday from me for $175 each – provided they were both in good condition. So we had two weeks use of pristine boards for 50 bucks each. What a lovely bloke. So if you're ever looking to hire or buy surfing, paddle-boarding or other water sports gear in Southern California, I recommend you making a beeline to Eric at Up Sports.

We decided to venture out the first day that the swell started coming in, when it was probably about eight to ten ft, but it was much too big for us – with the boards we had it was very difficult to get beyond the breaking water as it was nigh on impossible to duck-dive through and make ground. (Duck-diving is where you paddle at a wave and before it breaks on top of you, you point the nose of the board down and into the water, so that you go through the wave, rather than have it break on top of you or push you backwards). On the occasions we did manage to get over, it often had taken so much energy that we would need about 15/20 minutes to get our breath back, before actually starting to look for a wave.

However, there were successes, as on one occasion, in the midst of the swell, I caught what for me was a monster and had a superb ride – for the first time ever, I did a proper down the face, back up, down again, before I wiped out. I did get totally mashed by the broken water and didn't really know where I was until I finally came up for air, but the ear-to-ear grin answered any questions about whether it was worth it and was I all right. The next one tipped me straight in, treated me to a washing-machine-like, double 360 under the water, and so Harriet and I both agreed, "Hmm, yes, it's a bit big for us," so we headed to the shore, dumped the boards and went wave dodging instead. Suffice to say, though, our development was progressing nicely.

Being in these towns gave us access to some of the best surfing beaches in the area from Encinitas, Swami's, San Elijo and Carlsbad in the Oceanside area, up to San Onofre, Doheny and Trestles around San Clemente.

For us, our favourite beach was Doheny, where our spot was over towards the harbour wall, as the waves were consistent and not too menacing. On a number of occasions, we caught the same wave and having done our tricks and turns, were able to high-five each other whilst riding the wave before jumping off – a trick which earned us many a "Woop" from the beach.

Smiling usually happens after being in the water

8. OK, It's Time
25th March 2019

Jeez, it was cold that Sunday morning as I walked to the terminal at Edinburgh Airport – admittedly, it was 7 am and still quite early – but even so, it came as a shock. My last night at home had been really relaxing – pizza, beer and movie night where we watched *Four Weddings and Funeral*, which I hadn't seen in donkeys and Harriet had never seen. I'd forgotten what a great movie it is, laugh out loud funny, mixed with wry, subtle and occasionally caustic humour, leavened with the tear-inducing poignancy of the funeral and W H Auden ovation.

It never fails to amaze just how busy our airports are on Sunday mornings, as for some reason, I expect the world to be having their weekend lie-in, when the reality is that the snaking queues at check-in and security are the same day in day out as airlines operate the same schedule at weekends to those in the week. That said, I was in fortunate position that, thanks to airmiles, I had in my sticky-mitts a business class ticket and so was able to zip through security and into the lounge for a complimentary breakfast.

The short hop to Heathrow was brief, very smooth and uneventful, save for a near-miss incident which very nearly saw me wearing the in-flight supplied fruit salad, courtesy of the person sitting in front of me energetically going into battle with his seat reclining mechanism. Fortunately, the kiwi fruit, strawberries and melon slices by-passed me completely but did leave the empty seat next to me looking like BA had commissioned Jackson Pollock to do a redesign.

The flight to San Diego was on a 747 and for the first (and now probably last) time ever, on boarding I was invited to 'take the stairs to the upper cabin', which did make me feel a little embarrassed, but also I'll admit it, a little bit smug at the same time. There are only about 20 seats in Club World in the 'hump' so there is plenty of room to spread out I was spoilt for choice with extra storage bins to put all my gubbins in and – I know I could be wrong here – but it did seem as though some of the other customers had brough along extra stuff with them, just to ensure that they were able to fill their allotted bins. Maybe that's what Club Class is really all about – making sure you bring enough crap with you so that you're not embarrassed by the pitifully small amount of space you take up...?

Our departure was delayed by about two hours as during pre-flight checks, the pilots found a discrepancy between how much fuel the cockpit gauges reported was on board and how much the engineers had actually put in the tanks. It is fair to say that in many cases delays can cause a certain amount of angst and inconvenience, but for me, in this instance I was of the opinion that doing the due diligence to ensure that the plane had sufficient fuel onboard to actually get there was worth the wait, after all, filling up en route is not really an option when you're at 11,000 m or over Spitsbergen.

What a route it was though, cruising at that altitude on a clear day especially at this time of year, Greenland and Northern Canada were both still proper winter wonderlands, as it was possible to see the glacier-filled valleys running into the sea and the sea-ice was also still very much in evidence – breath-taking, awe-inspiring and fear-inducing in equal measure.

Is that The Wall from Game of Thrones…?

I made full use of the facilities on offer, excellent food (no seriously, don't laugh, it was really top-notch, a standing ovation was actually considered), an extremely well stocked bar, a seat which moved in almost every direction, depending on what comfort or position was required and of course, more movies/tv/music than you can shake a stick at. There was even a Club Pantry, where I could help myself to snacks, drinks and (yes, honestly) Wall's Magnums – comfort and ice cream, what more could I ask for?

After ten and a half hours of this, however, the plane landed and the spell was broken. Into the world of Homeland

41

Security we all wearily trudged, first to pick up luggage and then to the rubber glove line, I mean passport control.

For a brief moment I thought my luck was in again when one of my bags came out first, however, my hopes were cruelly dashed as I then had to wait until pretty much every other case had been picked up before my other one came out. Yes, yes, I know, I know, who needs two cases, blah blah blah – but I was going to be out here for nearly three months, so just one bag was never going to cut it. Anyhow, after a good hour, my passport got stamped, my retina were scanned and I was in California Boom! Made it!

Let the fun begin!

9. First Days
27th March 2019

Monday dawned bright and sunny – much as I'd hoped it would – and as I was jetlagged, being awake and up in time for my appointment with the waves was not a problem. Ahead of my trip, I had got in touch with Eric at Up Sports in Oceanside again to ask about getting some kit sorted out as well as booking some surf lessons and so it was there that I was headed for a 9 am start.

The town is about 20 miles south of San Clemente along Interstate Highway 5 and is an interesting blend of commuter town for San Diego, tourist hot spot for the beaches and support town for the army base at Camp Pendleton, which is just north of the town. The base is enormous, encompassing as it does c125,000 acres of beach, desert and mountain and is used for training and exercises primarily in desert warfare and sea-to-shore landing. Interestingly the Interstate Highway runs through the base, offering drivers the impressive – if slightly disconcerting – vision of charging tanks, swooping helicopters and amphibious craft converging on each other at high speed whilst you're on your way to work/surf.

I arrived at UP Sports just as the staff were opening up and met up with Carl, my instructor. I bought myself a new wetsuit (a 3/4 mm O'Neill, zipper-less one with sealed seams to keep it insulated, for anyone interested) and then headed with Carl down to the beach near the harbour, where we were to have the lesson. En route, he explained about the sorts of beaches close by, the ones that were better for less experienced surfers and the ones to avoid, all good and useful info for the forthcoming weeks, and more importantly for me the sort of detail it would otherwise take a long time to get hold of.

So, once we suited up and with the eight ft Wavestorm board provided tucked under my arm, we headed to the water. The sea temperature was fine – about 14 Celsius, which compares very favourably to the St Andrews and Dunbar's eight Celsius – and was consequently easy to adjust to. The waves were large-ish (five to seven ft) but smooth and with a slight offshore breeze, they were coming in at a consistent rate and pace. I paddled out beyond the breaking water to the line-up where 20 to 25 other surfers were waiting for their wave to come in. I gave it about 10 minutes to watch how the waves were coming in and see how everyone else was managing in the conditions and what sorts of techniques were being used.

I saw one coming in, and with no one else lined up, this was it, my first chance. I got down on the board, waited until the wave was about 15 feet from me and paddled as hard as I could. The board caught the wave, I felt the surge of speed as it took hold and propelled me forwards. Thinking I'd got it, I raised myself up and attempted to pop-up. I got to my feet, crouching low and then stood up. Unfortunately, my leading foot had forgotten where the board was and rather than being planted square in the middle, was way out on the left-hand side. The board veered to one side. I did an uncanny initial impression of a Weeble (remember those...?), but unlike they who wobbled but never fell down, I wobbled good and proper – and with not a little style I might add – and was then dumped firmly but decisively into the sea.

Carl was reassuringly brief and honest in his assessment, "Too early, man," followed by, "Gotta give it more time." Thus, knowledgably enriched, I headed back out to wait for the next one. Over the next 90 minutes or so, I paddled a hell of a lot, missed many waves, caught quite a few, fell off a lot but also rode several great waves to the beach. Most of the folk out weren't riding all the way in as it would have meant having to paddle back out much further afterwards, but given that they were catching many more than me, I couldn't really afford the luxury of disdainfully bailing on a ride I'd fought so hard to win.

The session was great, for the first time I caught a seven footer and when at the crest and faced with the vertiginous view down the board to the bottom, I managed not to panic, got myself up and raced down the face, turned, headed back up and just when I felt life was great, the wave broke on me and sent me tumbling down. I scrabbled around for a few seconds under the water, trying to find which way was up (no Yazz references, please) and bobbed to the surface with the biggest grin and loudest whoop of the day – whooping is allowed, by the way, and only frowned on by the hardcore. Returning to the beach, Carl gave me some instruction on how to improve my pop-up, as that was the area where most work was needed. He also asked if I was free on Wednesday morning for the lesson – to which I asked, "Well, what's this?"

His reply was that this was just an assessment to see what I needed and the lesson proper would be on Wednesday at 8 am. He also suggested I hung onto the board he'd provided me with for as long as I was here for or needed it, and when I pointed out I was here for two months and might need it for a long time, he was coolness itself – "Just give it back when you're ready." And with that, the session was done.

The next day I headed early to Doheny beach, which is about 10 minutes' drive north from San Clemente to practice what Carl had told me. The air temperature was colder and the waves not as big as the previous day (only about three ft) and there were only three other folk in the water when I arrived. However, what I quickly learnt was by positioning myself further up the board, this lifted the tail slightly, making it easier to catch the wave. It was a pretty fine line with this though, as if I lay too far forward the nose of the board submerged and I ended up face-planting into the water. That said, it was another good session, lots of new info picked up and by the time I got out, there were 20 or 30 folk in the water, so I felt I'd had the best of it.

I couldn't wait for the next day, back at Oceanside for the lesson proper...

10. The Lesson
29th March 2019

I met with Carl at 8 am by the same harbour beach at Oceanside as on Monday and chatted through how the previous day had gone and whether I'd been able to practice the pop-up. We got suited up, which in my case was rather gingerly as I had got a bit burnt soaking up the rays in the afternoon the day before – I was not really too sure how as I had put sun cream on, but either not enough or I'd been out in it too long and the effect was less bronzed god and more part-boiled lobster – not a hot look.

Just standing on the beach, I could tell the waves were a lot bigger – in the eight to twelve ft range – and so I was a little apprehensive; however, Carl thought they looked good and as he was in charge, who was I to disagree? Paddling out was quite difficult due to the incoming breakers, which kept trying to sweep me back to shore and made progress slow, however Carl showed me that by locating the rip current, it's possible (albeit with care) to use that to help you get out, as there are fewer breaking waves by it and its direction is naturally offshore.

It took a bit of time and involved several turtle rolls (where with an oncoming wave I would flip the board upside down, submerge myself while holding on and letting the crashing foam go over the top of me), but after about five minutes, we were sat on our boards, beyond the breaking water, moving gently in the swell and chatting to the other four or five folk out there. We didn't have to wait long for a wave to come in. I could see a good sized one approaching, so I got into position, started paddling and it simply passed me by. Missed it! OK, not a problem, wait for another. Next one came in, same thing, frantic paddling, wave builds, then passed underneath with barely even a hint it had noticed me. Damn! This was more difficult than I expected – I was thinking that with waves this size, I'd be cherry-picking them. Hmmm, rethink. Carl came over and said my paddling needed to be more focussed, by which he meant, 'You're thrashing about like an idiot, keep your strokes even and stop wobbling on the board.' Ah, OK. Method to the madness then.

With that in mind, I paddled back out and waited for the next one. A few came through in quick succession and so I watched some of the other guys to see how they got on. Of the five of them, only one caught the wave, the others had similar experiences to me in that the wave just passed under them without taking. *Hmmm,* I thought, *that is interesting, not just me then…*A few minutes later, I saw one approaching, got ready and started paddling in a more focussed manner. As it approached, I could feel the board being both pushed forwards and then as it got very close, sucked back towards it. This was not a good feeling. However, I didn't have long to ponder on this, as once the wave was at the back of the board, I felt it surge forwards, then start to lift, I popped up and looked down to make sure my feet were in the right place – they were. Yay! Unfortunately, I also looked beyond the board to the 12-foot drop down the face of the wave. "Aaaaggghhh!" That was a shocker. I wobbled, put all my weight on my back foot, which sent the nose of the board upwards, all momentum was lost, the wave crested, peaked and then broke directly on me. I did a 9.9 score cartwheel in the air, swiftly followed by a face-plant into the water and then was caught in the churning and roiling white water, where I did a submerged double 360 below the surface, before it washed over and spat me out so I could come up for air – a situation known as the *washing machine* as in: 'Was that you in the washing machine back there, dude?'

Much coughing, spluttering and some fairly robust industrial language ensued, but apart from being a little battered, I was very much undeterred and paddled back out – or at least that's what I tried to, but as I was now facing wall after wall of white water from the from the broken waves coming at me and not being in the rip current meant I was battling alone. 15 minutes later and very out of breath, I got back to the line-up and chatted as best as I could with Carl about what had just happened. I was pleased to hear that he was very positive about it ("You were close, but a bit late getting up") and offered a few more tips ("try pop-up earlier, weight further forwards, look ahead and not down" etc.). He also complimented me for going for a good-sized wave like that – "That would have put a lot of people off, dude."

The next couple of waves I missed, as they washed past me, and then the following one broke earlier than expected and nearly washed me straight off the board, which, with hindsight, might have been a better option. Instead, I stayed down flat and hung on to the board for dear life, legs flailing about like twigs in a storm. I could feel the power of the water surging all around me and as I didn't fancy another session in the washing machine, I just hung on in there, holding on as tightly as I could and let it carry me to the shore, where once I reached the shallows, I slid off the board and into the water, relieved not to have wiped out.

I sat on the beach for a wee while to get my breath back before venturing out again, and as I still couldn't locate the rip, it was a matter of paddle, turtle roll, thumped by a monster, get on board again, paddle, repeat. Another 15 or 20 minutes of this, and I was back out (bear in mind, this is probably only about 100m from shore, so not too a large a distance to cover…). I decided to wait a while before catching another to properly get my breath back and so that I'd be 'prepared'. I watched a few folks catch some great waves, but I was also rather relieved to see that for as many successes, there were as many misses and some pretty impressive wipe-outs as well. So, hmm, yeah, it was definitely not just me…

Having waited for 10 minutes or so, I felt it time to try again. A couple came by and I missed them, then I spotted what looked a likely wave one or two back, so I waited patiently, lined myself up and when it was about 20 feet from me, paddled like hell. It came at me at some speed, again, I felt the board surging forwards, but this time there was no pullback. I popped up to the crouching position, stared dead ahead and caught it. It was about 10 feet high and I was on the top of it. I glided down to the bottom, where it towered above me, a huge green menacing presence looming over. I didn't dare turn to look at it for fear of overbalancing, I just stood on the board, occasionally shifting my weight to make slight changes to where I was pointing. I purposefully tried no fancy stuff at all – turning up the face, changing direction, etc., as I knew that way would lie disaster. It was simply amazing. It felt like flying. I rode it all the way in, even after it had broken, I stayed on and got the 2nd and 3rd surges from it. I got a whoop from Carl and from a couple of people on the beach.

This was it. I had done it. First proper ocean break. Boom! Cue fist bumps and high fives.

Was I smiling? Happy? You betcha!

11. Out and About
1st April 2019

As I had surfed every day during the week, I felt a day off from the waves was called for, but not wanting to miss out on the weather and fresh air I still wanted to be outside. One of my favourite activities is walking, when at home the phrase 'Who's up for fresh air?' is one that many who know me will fully recognise; however, one of the challenges of American urban life is that because there is so much more available space, things are naturally a lot more spread out. So, whilst there may be 'local' shops, bars and restaurants, they tend to be a lot further away from residential streets and not necessarily grouped together in the manner which a Brit like me is used to. So this presents a problem. Whilst I'm happy to walk half an hour or so to the shops, I'm a little less keen then to walk back weighed down with all the shopping – you could perhaps call me a leisure-only walker. The solution to me seemed obvious – get a cheap 2nd or 3rd hand bike and use that while here and then either give it away or leave it for other folk renting the apartment once I was done.

I started with the town bike shop where they had a mountain bike which had been traded in the previous week by a local who wanted something else. It was a great bike. It had something like 21 gears, together with disk brakes, suspension and other fancy whatnots, and it was also the right size and was obviously in great nick. However, as it was priced at $270, which was fair if intending to keep for a long time, but as this was for just eight weeks it was pretty steep. It did also occur to me that for that sort of money, I could ditch the bike and get cabs or the bus instead, but that would be somewhat beside the point. I did ask about buying it now and then selling it back to him when I leave, which he was game for and suggested a buy-back price of $150, which was tempting, but in the end, I decided to move on and look elsewhere.

Hanging by the pier

The US equivalent of charity shops are called thrift stores, and there are quite a few of them in San Clemente on the main street, so it was there I headed next. These places had all the usual things I expected to find in a charity shop – clothes, books, CDs, pictures, DVDs, etc. – but were also a full-on Aladdin's cave of the truly bizarre, e.g. complete bathroom sets (bath, sink, khazi, even bidet – welcome back to the '70s!), other people's photo albums (perhaps you want to pretend someone else's holiday snaps are your own?), a TV remote control, the only accessory missing being the TV to use it with and umbrella stands (in this climate, really???). Baffling.

There was a lot of discarded sports equipment (many sets of golf clubs, scuba diving gear, beach tennis sets, etc.) as well, but a distinct lack of bikes. However, the last one I tried had a few parked outside and I thought my luck was in, so I checked them out. The first one had Easy Rider handlebars, which looked pretty cool (Raleigh Chopper, anyone?), but unfortunately had neither seat nor brakes, so that dropped it a few places in the ideal candidate list; the next was an '80s' style racer with dropped handlebars, bald tires, lots of rust and no gears and this being quite a hilly area and me being a bit of a lazy git meant this was discounted; the final one was in really good condition (seat, gears and brakes all present), but was bright fluorescent pink – even the wheels and tires were pink – and although not usually a colour snob (to which anyone who's seen my wardrobe can testify), I couldn't bring myself to purchase an object which might cause other road users to double-take and potentially swerve precipitously at me and so I passed on that one too.

So that left me without a bike, but still wanting to get out and about. Hmmm, what to do? As I was considering this, a couple of guys coolly swooshed past me on their skateboards – chatting freely, having fun and generally making good time along the way etc. Bing! Now that gave me an idea.

I got out my phone and googled "reconditioned skateboards San Clemente", and up came a store called Republik of Kalifornia, which happened to be just a block up the road, so that was where I headed.

On arrival I chatted with the extremely helpful owner, called Greg and explained my situation and requirements – I was staying for two months, I wanted to get out and about easily, no need for anything too fancy, happy to take a trade-in or whatever he recommended etc.

A few quick questions later and he had established my experience level, which as it consisted of having done a fair bit as a kid, done some on my children's boards and that I was used to balancing on a surfboard, which in total really added up to very little. However, undaunted, he said he was sure he could sort me out with something suitable and disappeared off into the storeroom, from where he brought out a 2ft board in the shape of a human foot which had square wheels on it. He put it on the counter and told me his plan was to take the wheels from this one and fix them on bigger board as that would be easier for me to ride – would that be ok? Now I'd be the first to concede that the extent of my physics knowledge is limited, however I do know that wheels which work well are circular, whereas wheels which are square do not and so I gave him a hard stare, frowned, scratched my chin and gave a loud "hmmmm". Greg asked me if there was a problem and as he was a large man who might not take kindly to being rebuffed, I cautiously ventured, "Well, sorry about this, I'm not trying to be funny, but the wheels, well, are they supposed to be square?" He looked from me to the wheels and back again and smiled as though dealing with an idiot, "They're not square, they're grooved." I looked again and agreed that they were indeed grooved, but they still looked square. He accepted that this was true but proceeded to say this was an optical illusion caused by the grooves and to prove it, he brought it round the counter, got on the board and went back and forth through the shop without no square-roll-juddering at all. He then explained that these were softer urban wheels and ideal for use on roads and paths as they enable the board (aka deck) to just roll over any stones rather than coming to a shuddering halt, face-planting me onto the ground.

That, I felt, was a reasonable enough explanation and so he went back into the storeroom and came back with a 3ft deck and built me a skateboard while I watched and that was how I re-joined the sk8er nation after a break of 30 odd years.

New wheels, dude

I know they look square, but honestly, they're not…

12. Weekend Break
2nd April 2019

Saturday morning dawned with a flawless clear sky, the sun was peaking over the horizon and it felt like time to take to the streets on the skateboard. As this was my first proper go, I decided to play safe and go somewhere flat, with a clearly marked cycle path, and separate from the road as traffic takes no prisoners here – especially along the coast road, which is the (in)famous PCH. The best place for this was down towards the beach where the footpath catered for both pedestrians and cyclists, it was completely detached from the highway by a metre-wide flower bed with hefty kerbstones, thereby providing plenty of deterrent to vehicles from encroaching and it also ran in pretty much a straight line between San Clemente and Doheny Beach. I took 10 minutes or so to have a few trial runs in the car park and to get a feel for how manoeuvrable and responsive it was, and once reassured that I could go, stop, turn, etc., it was time to be off.

The path is skateboarding heaven, super smooth, as it is essentially a tarmac extension of the road it runs alongside and despite a headwind, I quickly got the hang of it and started making good progress, fluidly turning to avoid any stones, sticks or other debris in my way – as this was in effect using the same skills to steer as those for surfing, which is really all about angling and turning your body to shift your weight from one side of the deck to the other.

I really enjoyed the perspective I got from gliding along the road, as it's one that differs greatly from that in a car, this was because I was able to look around much more and appreciate the scenery and houses that I was passing. Also, as this is a stretch with some of the most sought after (therefore read expensive) prime Orange County real estate there are some extraordinary beachfront properties to look at. One is built in the shape of three arks (of the Noah variety), with a large one pointing east-west towards the ocean, which makes up the ground floor and then has two smaller ones crossways on top forming the 1st floor. On the architectural scale, a smidgeon beyond bonkers maybe, but if you've got more money than you shake a stick at, why not? Whatever floats your boat – or ark I guess…

I wouldn't say I was travelling at tremendous pace, but I did manage to pass most of the runners who were out and I did pass all the pedestrians – I think I'd have packed it in there and then had I been overtaken by walkers. However, there were two hardcore runners who did manage to nip by me at one point – all tanned limbs, fancy shades and water bottle vests – but I rather pleasingly lapped them a mile further up the road, both bent double, breathing heavily and looking totally knackered – I gave them a wave and cheery 'Alright' as I glided by.

Unsurprisingly, it being the weekend and a glorious day, there were a lot of cyclists about, all of whom were going quicker than me, and my God, some of them were a sour-faced and silent bunch. All of the folk on foot – even the runners – would smile and pass a greeting, but apart from the leisure cyclists, the most I got from a very limited few of the speed merchants would be an infinitesimal nod of their helmeted and sunglass covered heads as they rocketed towards me and then schloofed by with a slap of slipstream; but most just ignored me as they seemed to with everyone. Why that should be, I couldn't tell, perhaps they felt their greater velocity made them a cut about the average bike/pedestrian lane user, quicker being superior, perhaps, and therefore us slower folk not worthy of acknowledgment. Whatever the reason, it seemed an odd way to behave.

My own personal theory was that it is caused by an overreliance on the manmade fibre and scourge of modern exercise – Lycra. What is it with cyclists and Lyrca? I can understand if you're Geraint Thomas or Laura Trott and that by wearing something sleek and figure hugging makes you more aerodynamic and not to mention go faster – which in their case, fair play, speed being key to their success and any small advantage over their rivals that they can get, be it training, breathing exercises or wardrobe, etc. they need to take. But weekend cyclists, will it help you get to the pie shop or pub any quicker? Come on, who are you kidding? I get that you may be cycling to get fit and healthy, very commendable and is to be applauded, but is it really worth doing that, looking like a poorly packaged bratwurst and then inflicting that look on the rest of us? I remain to be convinced.

Dude, know your limits!

Anyhow, I got to Doheny in once piece, having taken about an hour to cover the four and a half miles or so. I bought myself a long ice cold drink and triple scoop ice cream from the café (calories in to replace those expended…) while watching the surf action and reading the very guilty pleasure that is Viz. There were a lot of other attractions to observe as well, from beach volleyball to frisbee throwing and from kite flying to the groups of people playing football. Occasionally there would be a beaming toddler proudly showing off an ice cream which would then turn into disaster when the large scoop rolled off the cone onto the ground – quickly followed by much wobbling of lips and a frantic parental scramble back to the café for a replacement. I stayed and watched the world go by for about an hour before heading back and with the wind behind me, I was a bit quicker and so was back where I'd started in about 45 or 50 minutes. I'd had no spills, no wipe-outs and just the one near-miss, involving an ice cream, a tennis ball, a small dog and an arrestingly large and tattooed man who, to be fair to him, did accept full responsibility and assured me that he'd meant to throw the ball for the dog and not his Cornetto. The pained and wistful look he gave the rapidly melting mess was confirmation enough for me and on I went. A day very much chalked up in the Good column.

13. Waves for All
4th April 2019

The following day I was back at Oceanside to meet with Carl and a group of his friends, who run an adaptive surf club for people with disabilities called Waves4All, and he'd invited me to come along and help out for the day. I arrived there just after 8 am and it was already getting busy on the beach, with large friend and family groups having come for a day out by the ocean and who were setting up their BBQs; there were a lot of people who were out in the ocean to catch an early morning ride, as well as a varied assortment of beachcombers, walkers and the odd hobo here and there.

We set up the beach pavilion and put down rattan matting and tiles to enable wheelchair access from the car park across the sand and we also got a fire going in one of the pits provided. At about 9 am, a few folks started turning up at the pavilion and getting into their wetsuits and then we headed down to the water. The team have a number of boards specially made from a light and toughened polymer, with grab handles and a top surface which is rougher than the usual board, so that it provides extra grip. The first couple of folk lay on the boards and us helpers were there to work in relay to get them from the shore and out to the waves – someone at the shoreline to push out to waist depth, and then pass on to another helper with flippers on to paddle out. Once in the breaking water, we'd release the board and send them whooshing back to the beach, where the people in the shallows caught them and took them back out. Simple. Effective. Successful.

Whilst we were out in the waves, a number of other helpers arrived and set up tables laden with food, a great selection of subs, bagels, pastries, cupcakes, muffins – all perfect for keeping energy levels up – and during a lull in the early afternoon, I was able to get out and ride a few myself. So, all in all, a really great and satisfying day, lots of people got involved and there were many wanting to give it a try, from all walks of life – there were people with cerebral palsy, Down's, prosthetic limbs, visually impaired, etc.; a really inspiring day and the smiles said it all – riding waves makes you happy.

End of.

14. Interim Report
7th April 2019

After two full weeks I felt it was about time I took a more critical eye at how I was getting on and so I gave myself a brief progress review:

- **Ability**: Showing promise – I needed to read waves better so that more rideable ones are picked, as this would increase ride rate.
- **Technique**: Pop up definitely improved, as my feet were landing the in correct place a lot more often. My paddling needed to be less flailing about and more like focussed strokes; a fair bit of effort ought to be addressed to getting into position earlier and being

better aligned on the board so that less time was lost when lining up for a wave.

- **Style**: Hmmm, yes, OK. Let's move on for now.
- **Approach**: I needed to try to be braver and attempt for waves which may appear too big, as I may be surprised that they were not quite as ominous as they looked.
- **Enthusiasm**: Oh yes, got that in spades – it was more that I should work on channelling it better.
- **Grade**: C+

All in all, it had been a good first couple of weeks in the water, I felt that I'd definitely made progress with the pop-up, as I was falling off far less and staying upright for much longer without seesawing around. I knew my paddling was much stronger, as I could feel the board gliding better on top of the water with the nose dipping under less frequently. That said, there was clearly room for improvement in many areas, but looking at it positively, they're all areas that I could work on and there was certainly nothing which would make me (or hopefully anyone) shake their heads, suck their teeth and go, "Hmmm, have you thought about buying a frisbee…?"

Interim beach report:

Eight days at Doheny – the waves were quite small at the beginning of the fortnight but that helped me improve my paddling as I needed to do a lot more of it to catch the waves. On the later few days the swell was larger (which meant that the water being pushed to shore had more energy in it), this ensured that I caught some good rides but because the breeze was onshore it had the effect of flattening the waves as it pushed the peaks down.

Two Days Oceanside – here the surf was big and had strong rip currents which meant I only got beyond the breaking water a few times as the waves and current were too strong for me to get passed to the clean water. On one of the occasions that I did get out I caught a mean and nasty 7ft left (a left is when the wave breaks along the crest from left to right), which I caught and rode all too briefly before it collapsed on me, it shoved me right off side of the board and dumped me in the washing machine. After that, as I struggled to get back out again due to the repeated burying I was getting by the monsters, I decided to use time and energy better by staying inside and riding the broken water in order to practice my pop-up. (Waiting to catch a wave beyond the breaking water is called staying outside, catching broken waves is called staying inside).

Two Days at San Onofre – I'd been warned that this beach can be very territorial, with some surfers being aggressive both verbally and physically to people they think are on their turf (as it were), kooks (inexperienced surfers – i.e. me) especially being a target for their wrath, so I had been a little wary about going there. In truth though, apart from a few younger guys where there was a bit of macho posturing of the "stay out of my way" kind – which I was more than happy to do anyway – it was hardly intimidating. I paddled on passed the posse and found a spot in the line up a bit further down where there were a few women and a couple of older guys who were all shooting the breeze and quietly mocking the "crew" at the other end. Anyway, the waves were superb, far and away the best that I'd had on the trip so far – there was a slight offshore breeze (which pushes the face of the wave up making it crest later), a strong swell and regular sets coming in (a set is a group of three or four good surfable waves which come in one after the other). This meant that there were plenty of waves for everyone, my ride rate increased to 50% (i.e. I caught every second wave that I went for) and I was able to glide down, turn and ride back up the wave on four or five occasions. It was without doubt my best day yet on the water and I resolved to be back at San Onofre again quite a lot over the coming weeks. All in all, a good fortnight's work.

Oceanside harbour break

San Onofre – miles and miles of breaks

15. Playing Ball
11th April 2019

Whenever I've been here in the summer, Major League Baseball (MLB) games have very often been showing on TV and having watched it for a while with a beer or two, it's been entertaining to watch, as it's a fairly quick game with a good amount of action, but as I don't know the rules, I've never really understood why certain things happen and what a lot of the dialogue means. I happened to mention this to one of the people I'd met in the pub on an earlier night, and before I knew it, I'd been signed up to go see a ballgame with a lady called Donna, who (at least as far as I was concerned) happened to be something of a baseball expert.

Before we get into the game, I should say a few words about Donna. She was one of those people it was always a pleasure to be around as she always had a good story to tell and being an Italian American – originally from Boston – she had a very European sense of humour, never short of a fast quip or good old-fashioned sarcastic remark. I'll return to Donna and her friends later, but for now, we shall look go back to the baseball.

There are two teams local to San Clemente – the Padres, who play in San Diego, and the Los Angeles Angels, who play in Anaheim. The Padres are so called, as it's in reference to the Spanish Franciscan friars, who founded San Diego in 1769 and the Angels because their stadium used to be in downtown LA (the City of Angels) – thank you, Wikipedia but is now in Orange County, although they retain the LA name.

Angel Stadium

Donna recommended that we should go and watch the Angels because they're pretty good, they had a run of home games coming up and as the stadium is close to the railway station, we would avoid the Orange County (OC)/LA rush hour on the freeway – all sound reasons, and given I had no knowledge of any of the above and having no desire to fight freeway traffic, there was no argument from me.

So, we got our tickets booked, turned up at the OC Metrolink station in San Clem and headed off. The train was a bit of a treat as it happened that it follows the coast for a good while, and as the carriages are double decker, the view out of the windows is excellent. It was quick, clean, on time and with friendly staff, all somewhat unusual in fact for any regular user of UK rail – especially ScotRail…

True to Donna's word, the station was indeed five minutes' walk from the stadium (any football/cricket/rugby team owners reading this, please take note – building a stadium for your team in the middle of nowhere does not help your fans get access it via public transport, while the land maybe cheap, your customers' trek to and from will be arduous and frustrating). The capacity of Angel Stadium is around 45,000, which makes it larger than average of the Major League Baseball grounds, but someway smaller than the largest – which happens to be the stadium of their nearest neighbours/rivals, the LA Dodgers, which can accommodate 56,000 Angelenos.

Just before the game started, the national anthem was sung and then it was straight into the action. Donna kept me fully briefed on why such and such was happening or why so and so did something, however I shan't try and explain everything, but I now understand how a batter can face up to seven balls before he's either:

1. Out due to three misses – the legendary three strikes and you're out rule, or
2. He's walked – where the pitcher throws four duff pitches and the batter therefore gets to 1st base without hitting a ball, or
3. He hits the ball and he gets to one of the bases because he's hit it sufficiently far to make it – or in the case of hitting it over the boundary (don't know if that's the

correct word…), where he can run round 1st, 2nd and 3rd to Home Base which is why that's called a Home Run.

There are nine innings for each team and to get a team out, the fielding side need to get three batters out and then they swap over and at the end of the nine innings, the team with the most runs wins. Whilst nine innings sounds a lot of game time – and I suppose in some ways it is – there's more than enough action for it all to move along at a fair clip and so the two and half hours that the game took went by quite quickly. Having seen America Football and Ice Hockey in action I was very impressed that the changeovers were conducted so speedily – five minutes max for batting team to come out to field and for the fielding team to get batting – and there were only a minimal number of breaks for "Words from our sponsors".

There were three home runs in the game, some pretty impressive running catches and lightning fast fielding, all of which got the crowd on its feet a lot. It ended 5-2 to the Angels, which meant the home crowd went home happy and the team maintained its then six game winning streak – the season had only started about a fortnight before, so it was a bit early to be thinking about a tilt at the World Series, but it was looking good at that point.

The biggest news of the evening – and it certainly got the biggest cheer – was the announcement that Mike Trout, their star batter and fielder (and local boy), had just signed to stay with the Angels for his whole career. Apparently, it was the largest baseball contract ever awarded and was worth $426m to him; which at the very least will keep him in caps, gloves and chewing gum for some while…

There was a great atmosphere throughout the game, with as much respect shown to the away team for good play as the home team, and as with all American sports, the food and drink was front and centre. There were the guys walking the aisles with drinks, ice creams, churros, sweets etc. and a particular highlight for me was the 'large nachos with trimmings' which is amusingly served in a baseball helmet and at a guess would provide a family of five with at least a three days' worth of the recommended sugar, salt and fat intake. I'd recommend checking you've finished eating before trying it on for size.

Would sir like a chinstrap with his dinner?

16. Giving a Little Back, Part I
14th April 2019

When I was doing the planning for my trip, one of the things I wanted to avoid happening was ending up spending eight weeks or so surfing and then just being in the apartment on my own. I felt strongly that as I had this fantastic opportunity, I should make the very most of it, to get out and meet people and if possible, try and get involved in the community. I wasn't entirely sure what that would entail or even how I'd go about achieving it, but it seemed an important aim to have.

So, ahead of travelling, I searched online for voluntary organisations in the San Clemente area who were looking for people to help out and found a couple of email addresses of potentials. I contacted them to say I was going to be in the area for eight to 10 weeks, from March to May and if they were agreeable, I'd like to work for them for some of the time I would be out there. The first to respond was a guy called Branden Earp, who works for an organisation called Family Assistance Ministries (FAM) and who are based on a business park on the outskirts of town. Brandon replied to say that they were always looking for people to get involved and that they had a variety of activities coming up where I would be welcome to assist and that I should get in touch when I had arrived. I also asked about work permits etc. as I didn't want to find myself on the wrong end of a Trump-inspired removal of undesirables, Branden looked into it and confirmed that as this was voluntary work with no pay etc., then there would be no issue. All good.

Family
Assistance
Ministries

Having arrived in San Clemente, I got back in touch and went round for an orientation session at the FAM warehouse with some of the team working there and learnt a good amount about what they do and how etc. Essentially FAM provided assistance to families and single folk who were struggling to make ends' meet in today's America and who might have needed a helping hand to get back on their feet. This could be folk who had been made redundant and were between jobs with bills to pay, people whose relationships had broken down and suddenly had no place to stay or people on low incomes whose salaries did not stretch quite far enough to cover all the monthly outgoings etc.

One of their primary operations was a large food bank which functioned rather like a supermarket, whereby their clients came by and could get a huge range of everyday essentials. This covered fresh fruit and veg, through bread, cakes, biscuits, dairy and all the fish/meat types to frozen produce, as well as a full variety of non-perishable goods, such as pasta, rice, tinned food, jam and peanut butter. They also provided toiletries, nappies and other necessary household goods which everyone needs in order to live a normal life. All of these were supplied either at low cost or free from organisations, such as Second Harvest, which is a federal government food bank service, local supermarkets and in a unique relationship they had partnered with Starbucks to pick up all the unused fresh food they do not sell on a daily basis.

The amount of food they were able to get hold of was staggering – and without trying to overwhelm with facts and figures – on average, most US households threw away roughly 40% of the food they had bought, uneaten. I don't know what our percentage is in the UK, but given that our society functions along similar lines it may well not be all that different. Quite a sobering thought.

It was a reasonably large organisation, their warehouse used to be a four-engine fire station and from this they were able to help a huge number of families in the South Orange County area – and actually very surprisingly to me – one of the largest groups of people they helped were the soldiers and their families just down the coast at Camp Pendleton. This was because the salaries of many of the newest recruits and lower level troops were not always high enough to provide for everything they needed – especially not when taking into account the higher taxes paid in California. It presents quite a juxtaposed position if we were to look into how much a helicopter costs or if that amount is spent on developing, building and testing missiles, or a tank being driven ten miles would use however much fuel, and then to compare that to the salaries for the men and women on the front line and see which is the better use of resources. However, as I don't have all those facts, I can't really get into a full and frothy rant about it. But what I can tell you is that it was a fact that a significant number of those soldiers and their families were increasingly dependent on receiving food given to them by FAM. Hmmm, America, not all what you expect…

Anyway, I was set to work, sorting out the bakery stuff, fresh fruit and veg and dairy, ready to be given out and then I moved into the foodbank/supermarket area, where I helped fill the trollies of a number of clients with food for them to take away. There were some rather tasty looking chocolate cakes, which went quickly, as did the steaks, milk and enchiladas. The fruit and veg was also snapped up, although I wasn't able to convince anyone to take any of the courgettes and aubergines, until I asked one of the other helpers why that might be, and they politely told me – "That's because they have no idea what you're talking about – to us those are zucchini and eggplant." Having corrected my grocery vocabulary, I was giving them away like hot cakes.

It was a great day and it felt good to be able to help out. I met some lovely people and I was invited back to help again, provided I started saying toh-may-toh rather than to-maah-toh. Britain and America, eh? Two nations divided by a common language…

Just before I headed off, I was asked if next time I'd fancy going on a ride-along with the trucks which pick up the food early in the morning to bring back to the warehouse and being an overgrown kid, my response was along the lines of, 'Ooh, ooh, ooh, yes! Yes! Pick me! Pick me! Pick me!'

17. Surfing Safari
17th April 2019

A few weeks into the trip and I was joined in San Clemente by Harriet and Alex, who were on Easter break from school and Uni respectively. It was a real treat to have them both stay, not only for their excellent company, but also that special laughter and joy that your children always bring, plus it was also cool that they are both keen surfers.

Ahead of Alex's arrival, Harriet and I decided to have a day away from the waves and headed to the San Diego Wild Animal Park, which is owned and run by the San Diego Zoo. It's located about 30 miles inland of the city, over nearly 2000 acres and has 50 different species in large enclosures, which are all built to resemble each animal's habitat.

The park is spilt into two distinct sections:

1. A series of trails and looped paths, which enable visitors to walk around the outside of the enclosures and observe the animals up close, via the various viewing galleries.
2. The African Plains tour, which is an open-air trolley ride around the open 800-acre park, which has many of the largest animals roaming free and has tree and plant species native to the savannah.

Savannah in Southern California

Both are very well done and well laid out, making it easy to navigate around the different zones and see all of the animals. First up were the gorillas, whose enclosure has a combination of trees, climbing frames, water, grass and rocks both to climb and also to shelter within. They have a big silverback male, three adult females, one of whom had recently given birth to two babies as well as a number of adolescents of both sexes. Whilst we were there, there was a whole lot of action in progress – play-fighting, climbing the rocks and frames, as well as some major feeding.

There are lion and tiger enclosures with up to five of each species in them; the Sumatran tiger enclosure is especially impressive, as it comprises three zones, one of which has a cooling waterfall and another includes a pool as these cats love water – which debunked a myth I'd always had that all felines have an intense dislike for water. As for the lions, the big male was nowhere to be seen, as we discovered from a keeper that he was asleep in a tree, while the females were entertaining the cubs – familiar-sounding behaviour, anyone...?

No tapping the glass please, this kitty bites!

After stopping for our picnic, we took the trolley ride around the African Plains, where there were giraffes, gazelles, antelopes, wildebeest, zebras, rhinos and emu roaming freely about as they all seemingly live in harmony, just as they do on the savannah. We were privileged to see two baby giraffes, who had only been born the week before and were still in the giraffe house. The word baby is of course relative in this context, as both were roughly six foot tall when born. Bet that makes your eyes water a bit…

Aww, look at the 'little' babies…

As is often the case, it was the elephants who were the scene-stealers. Spread over roughly 150 acres, there are two large enclosures for the herd, a few of whom were rescued from being culled in Swaziland, as part of a government initiative in 2003, and since their arrival, six calves have been born. There is a large pond for them to enjoy a cooling swim, as well as shade structures made from simulated rock, and given the size of the enclosure, there is oodles of room to roam.

I know that zoos and safari parks often come in for criticism (and quite rightly in some cases, where the animals are clearly not being well cared for), but I put the San Diego Wild Animal Park and its sister Zoo firmly in the positive category. Whilst they are obviously a commercial enterprise, their ethos is care and wellbeing for the animals they look after. They are involved in many conservation programmes with governments, other zoos and organisations around the world. At present, they're working to bring the Northern White Rhino back from extinction by using two of their Southern White Rhino females as surrogates, which hopefully once born and at a suitable age, can be released into the wild.

One Rhino post-mud bath, the others will take theirs later

Another example is the Arabian oryx, which is an antelope native to the Arabian Peninsula and Sinai Desert that due to hunting had become extinct in the wild by the late 1960s. In 1972, they joined Operation Oryx, which was a programme set up to save it from extinction and since then almost 400 have been born at the park, many of which have returned to Oman and Jordan to be reintroduced to the wild.

However, whatever your feelings regarding these institutions, Harriet and I came away very impressed by what we'd seen and learnt, they have some really beautiful animals in the park, all of which appear to be thriving.

18. Caught on Film
19th April 2019

During Alex and Harriet's visit I finally plucked up the courage to take Harriet's GoPro waterproof camera out with us, as up to this point I'd not felt confident enough to catch and ride waves whilst filming at the same time, and to be perfectly honest I would probably have continued to put it off again and again if Alex hadn't suggested we try it.

So off Alex and I headed to Doheny again (Harriet having flown back to the UK the previous day), this time in the late morning so the sun would have had time to warm up the water a wee bit. The waves looked good from the beach and so it proved, as we were now getting swell from the Southern Pacific, bringing warmer water from the equator and Mexico. The currents of the world's oceans change according to the seasons, and so up until earlier this week, we had been getting waves from the north, but now they were from the south and would be until the end of summer.

We paddled out to catch a few and get our eye in for the session, then I went and got the camera, which is a really cool piece of kit. It's cube-shaped and roughly four cm each side, fully waterproof (well, we hoped it was) with a mounting so it can be fixed to bikes, helmets, boards etc. However, as the boards we're using aren't ours, I couldn't really fix it to one of those, but, I did have a lanyard which I attached and then decided that the best place to hold it was by gripping the mounting in my teeth – aye, I know, loss of teeth a possibility, loss of dignity a certainty – but I didn't really have any other options as I needed my hands to paddle…

It turned out to be really straightforward. We got lined up, turned on the camera, paddled, caught a wave, rode it in, stopped filming and whooped (where appropriate, of course…).

Back at the apartment, I uploaded the footage. As you'd expect, there were plenty of clips of us falling off and showcasing the watery side of the ocean, but in between, there were a few gems which we were both really pleased with.

19. Ladies Who Lunch
22nd April 2019

In an earlier chapter I mentioned Donna who had taken me to the baseball game. I had met her on a night out at a bar just up the road from where I was staying called Iva Lee's early on in my trip and we got to know each other pretty well through a shared passion for live music, good food and a few drinks. On a couple of occasions, she invited me to join her and her friends for lunch at the Fisherman's Bar on the pier at San Clemente. Daniela, Nancee, Barbara and Debbie were a lovely group of ladies, very friendly and welcoming and didn't seem to mind at all me gate-crashing their meet ups. In addition to the excellent food at The Fisherman's Bar, they also had a really good cocktail happy hour, which started at three pm and ran on until about six, which always provided plenty of time for chat, soaking up the sun and general relaxation.

Usually after a lunch the ladies would peruse the shops in San Clemente – Donna was keen on the thrift stores as she has a very good eye for glass and can spot a really good piece at a hundred paces – Murano being a speciality. I tagged along to several of these sessions – I wasn't buying anything, but the laughs were loud and frequent and I was often quite useful in the "Would you mind holding this?" or "You couldn't reach that for me, could you?" department.

One afternoon I got a message from Donna to meet her at the harbour in Doheny as there was a surprise in store and not having any other plans in place, I was only too glad to go along. I met her at Pier 9 and when I asked what we were doing there, she told me we were just in time to board a boat for a whale and dolphin watching trip. These trips are run on a regular basis during the day and last for a couple of hours, while they head a few miles out to sea, where bottlenose, common and Risso's dolphins swim, and also where blue and grey whale were currently migrating north to their cold-water feeding grounds of Canada and Alaska.

Three miles out, we came across a pod of about 70 common dolphins, who, having located a shoal of fish, were corralling it so that they could all feed. I was transfixed, watching them work together, darting about over an area of roughly half a square mile for 15 or 20 minutes corralling the fish into a smaller and smaller area so that they could all then feed. I know that with the recent nature documentaries many of us will have seen this sort of thing captured on film, but to be able to witness it happening in front of me was something else altogether. Breathtaking.

I greatly enjoyed all the time I spent with Donna and her gang, as they were generous with their friendship and time and they helped me feel a little bit part of their world, which when I was a long way from home, not knowing any people at all was a something to be cherished.

20. Not All About the Waves
24th April 2019

Whilst Alex and Harriet were here, we took a few days off from the ocean to do some sightseeing – absolutely no point travelling all that distance and not taking in some of the other attractions available, after all. So on one occasion, we followed the coast road from Oceanside down towards San Diego, which passes through a number of beach towns, which vary from gated communities with multi-million-dollar beachfront pads for the local super-rich to others, which look as though they've barely changed since the '60s when they were colonised by artists, hippies and dropouts. I'm not sure about you, but I much preferred the latter as they were more open, welcoming and pleasant to see than the seemingly clinically divorced from real life world of the mega-mansions…

'Let's just lie by the pool today'

It took about an hour to get to La Jolla (pronounced La Hoya), which is a wealthy and well-to-do suburb of San Diego, about five miles north of the city. On the face of it, there's nothing particularly special about it, there are a lot of posh-looking restaurants and high-end designer boutiques, which would not be out of place in the upmarket areas of London, Paris, Rome, and are very much of the type that I can never see myself ever frequenting…But once you leave the town centre and head to the cliffs overlooking the ocean, there are two real wonders in store. Firstly, all along the two miles or so of coastline there are rocks and coves which have been completely colonised by sealions, so much so that in some places there is barely a square metre free. The second wonder is that they are totally at ease with the presence of humans, to the extent that when they're lying on the sand and rocks sunning themselves, you can stand or sit within a metre of them and they completely ignore you, as though you weren't there. It's truly remarkable. Added to that the flocks of California Grey Pelicans, which cruise about above you in aerobatic flight formation and you get a real sense of closeness to the natural world.

On another occasion, Alex and I went inland up into the foothills of the Santa Rosa mountains to Anza Borrego Park, which is located in the Colorado Desert of southern California. Its name comes from 18th century Spanish explorer Juan Bautista de Anza who 'discovered' it and 'borrego', the Spanish word for sheep as the park is home to Long Horn Sheep. Until a few weeks prior to our visit due to the unusual amount of winter rain which had fallen, there had been a great deal of brightly coloured wildflowers growing all over the park, however, as spring was well underway by the time, we were there with daytime temperatures not much below 27 or 28 degrees Celsius, most of them had by now disappeared. This is very much a place of extreme heat as is in July and August, the average temperature is 40 to 42 degrees Celsius, so when visiting a lot of caution and lots of water are essential.

One of the park highlights is a three-mile round trip hike up Palm Canyon, which follows the course of a mountain stream to where a natural spring emerges from the ground, forming an oasis and which provides enough water for a grove of 40 to 50 full size palm trees to grow. The walk was not very arduous and clearly marked but should definitely not be undertaken without plenty of water and at least trainers on your feet. A ranger at the start of the hike trail was advising visitors that a rattlesnake had been present earlier in the day and to exercise appropriate caution should you see it (poking with a stick to 'get an action shot to show Grandma' is not one which comes recommended). The walk took us about two hours in total, and we did get pretty hot and tired, but once we arrived at the oasis, it was very much worth it as the tranquillity and peace, together with the natural coolness which comes with there being water and a breeze made it a wonderfully calming place.

At the oasis, there was a lot of water spilling down the rocks and into the stream, but as we followed the walk back down, it was interesting to see how little of it actually made it to the bottom as it began to evaporate in the increasing seasonal heat. We were pleased not to come across the advertised rattler and equally pleased to see a good number of the big horned sheep about 20 feet above us on the hillside, who were perhaps watching to make sure we left their home in an orderly and undisturbed state, a very fitting end.

'Ere, no messing up my gaff, you hear?'

21. Half Term Report
26th April 2019

Having reached what was roughly the halfway mark of my trip, it was time for another assessment of where I was up to. As I had spent much of the time at Doheny and San Onofre beaches with only one trip to Oceanside, I felt it best to focus on those two locations.

San Onofre – every time I had visited, there had been really great swell coming in and I managed to catch many of the breaks I went for. There were some really smooth six or seven ft crests, with lots of gliding down the face and back up and as high tide approached, with the wave energy dropping in readiness for the tide to turn I had learnt that by careful shifting of the feet and weight, I was able to dip the nose sufficiently for the board to keep catching the swell and ride to shore again. This had been particularly pleasing, as it meant that I now had the ability to control the board better, enabling me to steer it properly and maintain momentum. There was just the one incident to report.

- On one early morning session, while I was out waiting for my wave scanning the horizon with my 2000-yard iceman stare, I thought I caught a glimpse of a dorsal fin. I shook my head to clear my eyes and when I refocussed it had gone and so I put it down to a case of the surfer's equivalent of 'cabin in the woods fear' and resumed my search. About two minutes later, I saw it again, but this time, it wasn't one, but two dorsal fins, both of which very definitely crested and then submerged; they then turned around and went by me the other way. To say that my attention was grabbed, barely hints at the wild scenarios being played out in my head and I looked about to see if any of the other folk out had seen them, but no-one appeared to have noticed. So I paddled as smoothly as possible over to a couple of guys and as quietly and slowly as possible asked them if they'd seen the fins. They both looked at me like the kook I clearly was and one of them calmly said, "It's dolphins, dude. Just dolphins."

I tried (and undoubtedly failed) to retain an air of nonchalant detachment, and replied, "Oh, yeah. Cool, thought so." Pause. "Get many of them here?"

To which I was informed, "Yeah, quite a lot, they're pretty cool, just doing their thing." Pause. "You go a bit further out, you might see grey whales, they're migrating right now to the arctic to feed."

At that point, I felt I'd been educated enough in the presence and habits of the local sea life and gave them a lowkey, "Cool," and paddled off. After about 10 minutes, my heartbeat had slowed sufficiently to enable me to breathe in and out normally again and resume my flint-eyed glaze for the next wave.

Doheny – with the exception of a couple of flattish days, the waves had been pretty consistent – three to four ft when cresting and good levels of energy – meaning that there were good opportunities to catch and ride, provided I paddled hard enough – so that's where most of my practice had been

g Department

Children, Edinburgh

mation Sheet

be helpful for you to keep

to drink lots of fluid for the next 24hours

department on 0131 536 0268

/55

Burpathlon

①
3 × 10 (30 sec's Rest

3 × 10 (30 sec's Rest
(10 mins

60 secs Rest

② Cycle 10 km (30 mi
(2 × Braids Road)

③ Run 3 × KB loop
(5 km) (30 m

focussed...As a result, my paddling had improved to the extent that I could consistently catch the waves before they broke. Couple of incidents to report:

- Having got out to the line-up on another early morning, I was quietly minding my own business, waiting for my wave when a turtle surfaced directly next to my right leg – I don't know the correct terminology to describe turtle size, but "whopper" fitted the bill. Its shell was – at a guess – 60 to 80 cm in diameter, its head and neck were about 15 to 20 cm long, its eyes were large and black and its mouth was wide open. I don't know which of us was the more surprised, as I've not seen enough turtles to know if 'startled' looks much different to 'meh, another on a board'. As it happened once it had heard my, "Yikes! That's a surprise" (or words to that effect), it dived under and swam away, leaving me to resume my search for a wave. About ten minutes later, another surfer paddled by and told me I should be careful as a snapping turtle had been seen and it would think nothing of helping itself to a toe or other available appendage within reach of its jaws...

- Towards the end of another particularly good session, I had planned to head in after my next wave and once I had caught it, I rode it to the shore and in a bid to look cool and in control, I tried to casually step off the board onto the beach. However, I somewhat mistimed this as I was knocked forwards by another incoming wave right behind me, which catapulted me forwards and I face-planted onto the sand. Ahem, feigning an insouciance I really did not feel, I got up, brushed myself off and headed back out for just one more, just as I had really intended…

Ability: There was a definite improvement here, my wave selection had got much better as the ride rate was higher.

Technique: My pop-up had got much snappier (turtles aside), as I was landing my feet 60 to 70% of the time correctly, reducing the wobble as I tried to adjust; My paddling was much stronger and more coordinated, therefore giving me better power to catch. Further work was definitely needed though on pop-up, as sometimes I unbalanced the board and end up in the drink.

Style: Not on the catwalk yet, more like watching from the wings.

Approach: I had got bolder with wave choices, but definitely needed to pluck up the courage and try for the larger beasts, as even if I missed them, I would be picking up info for future.

Enthusiasm: Certainly, no dips here, still very much full-on – perhaps less haste, more speed, as a former teacher once put it to me.

Best Day: This was a very recent session, when I had caught 13 of the 15 waves I went for – that's a pretty good ride rate there.

Grade: B-

My next test was to be a further session with Carl, the instructor who had sourced a shortboard that he wanted me to try – this was potentially my ticket to the big leagues and would be where it could get interesting …

22. Retail Therapy
29th April 2019

I have never been a big fan of clothes shopping as I find it pretty tedious and pointlessly time consuming. In days gone by when I went to buy clothes, I would usually go into the first shop and find something I liked, but not buy it, as I wanted 'to see what everywhere else had going'. I'd then spend the next (let's say) two hours traipsing around all the other clothes shops, looking at near-identical items and comparing them to what I'd seen in the first shop and usually comparing them unfavourably. Once I'd exhausted all the options – not to mention the patience of anyone with me and/or shop staff – I'd pretty much always end up back in the original shop, buying what I'd seen when the trip began.

Since then my approach to buying clothes has evolved. When my children were young and time and attention spans were short (and not just the children's, I should add…), the whole shopping around thing just wasn't feasible and so if I wanted jeans, for instance, I would go into just one shop and look at what was there, I might try on a pair or two and if the feeling I got was, 'Hmm, yeah, they'll do,' I'd buy them and go home; but if the feeling was more, 'Hmm, nah, maybe not,' I would usually just call it a day there and then and go home and save myself the bother.

On a very rare occasion, I might visit a second shop and repeat the above, but that would only be in exceptional circumstances (i.e. an urgent need for new clothes either because the current ones had fallen apart or something was needed for a special occasion). I stuck with this approach for a fair amount of time until the last few years, when I modified it again to being simply going to the shop where I know they have what I want and so therefore I can cut out the fannying about part of considering where to go or even looking elsewhere. This explains why I get shirts from Charles Tyrwhitt, suits from Sparks (not that I wear one very often), Levi jeans and rugby shirts from House of Fraser (Howick) – although I think these have now fallen by the wayside post the Mike Ashley takeover, so I may have to find a new source for these. For anyone familiar with my sartorial style over the years, the above will no doubt provide some enlightenment along the lines of: 'Oh, right! That's why he was still wearing that.' In short, for me, time spent shopping for clothes is time wasted when it could be much better expended on doing something you enjoy.

So it came as something of a major surprise to find myself at the Mission Viejo shopping mall and actually enjoying walking round, browsing shops, interacting with people and generally seeing what was available. I'm not entirely sure what brought this on, as it's a huge place with about 160 shops, including two branches of Macy's department store and with a seemingly endless array of similarly looking shops, however. I expect my improved shopping mojo could have been for any or all of the following.

1. The feeling of space and – believe it or not – tranquillity, as there was no muzak, but plenty of natural light.
2. There were no screaming kids or groups of yoof barrelling along the concourse.
3. The place had comfortable seats to rest up in and take a break between shops.
4. It had a food court which served decent food.

Whatever it was, it all added up to make the whole experience a great deal more enjoyable than I had expected.

You may be wondering what I ended up buying, well as it happens, I bought nothing but I did have some fun in the

Tommy Bahama shop, where they sell "beach and leisure wear" mostly bearing palm and coconut tree prints to people for whom the need for attire emblazoned with wild patterns allied with a strong blend of primary colours would appear to a clinical necessity. Now, don't get me wrong, I myself do own a boldly coloured shirt or two, which are brought out on special occasions, but I struggle to see just how big a market there is for linen trousers covered in technicolour palm trees, which are then paired with shirts, adorned with sandy beaches and pina coladas (you could also have waves rolling into the shore) and as a piece de resistance, why not top it all off with a pork-pie straw hat, replete with beach umbrella motifs. As a statement of one's wardrobe choices, it's brave and it's bold – and how do I know this? Well, in the spirit of being a consumer champion I tried them all on. All at the same time. It was awful. It was grotesque. It was buttock-clenchingly bad. I really couldn't believe anyone would ever want to buy any of this stuff, but I was clearly in the minority with this view as they were doing a roaring trade, which I guess explains why I never had that big career in fashion.

On the way out back to the car I had a brief encounter with a different type of sales technique as I was stopped by a lady selling 'beauty products for men'. She handed me a sachet of some jollop to make my hair either less this or possibly more that, I don't remember which, but no doubt it would do something to my hair which it really did not need doing. She then proceeded to talk really quickly and at some length about how there were 'excellent products for a guy like you to make your skin feel like your skin again'. Now to be perfectly honest, I can't say I have ever thought that my skin felt like someone else's, but I let it pass. During a brief pause in the sales pitch, I told her it wasn't really my thing to which she moved seamlessly on to asking me what my current exfoliating regimen consisted of; I'm assuming my answer of "salted peanuts and pale ale" is not a technique known in Orange County as she had no response at all, which did at least give me the chance to make my escape.

23. Better Waves = Better Filming
2nd May 2019

Following my lesson with Carl, I had a good few days using the shortboard and trying to capture more film footage.

I was really pleased with how I got on with the shortboard as it is notoriously difficult to get the hang of, as it was a lot more agile and moved much more quickly and consequently was a lot less stable. Best comparison would be if a longboard were a BMW X5 (chunky, gets the job done, no fuss, dependable), the shortboard would be its cheeky younger sibling the BMW Z4 (zippier, instant fun, not for everyone). Apologies for the car analogy and also if it does not make any sense to you. However, simply put, the shortboard was really hard work, because:

- A lot more paddling was required.
- It took quite a while to learn where the sweet spot was to stand on the board.
- I found that it was only really effective in conditions where the waves were larger and peakier.

- The rides you get are much shorter as they run out of steam a lot quicker.

That said, I persevered with it as I wanted to try and master the skill, but it didn't return nearly as much fun for me as the longboard. Once it became clear though that the waves were going to be smaller for a while I switched back as it enabled me to keep riding and also to get more footage. Which I was getting quire adept at capturing.

24. Giving a Little Back, Part II
4th May 2019

In an earlier chapter , I wrote about the work I had been doing as a volunteer at the Family Assistance Ministries (FAM) in San Clemente, helping out in the food bank warehouse with whatever was needed and I finished the story, having been asked to help out on the morning ride-along in one of the trucks to pick up the food from the supermarkets.

The big day arrived and as Alex was still staying, I had cleared it with Jeff, the warehouse manager, for him to join in as well. In case you're wondering whether I had press-ganged Alex into this, I can assure you that that was not the case, as he had asked if it would be possible to come along.

So, we rocked up at the warehouse at 7:30 and were allocated to help Doug, who was driving the old U-Haul truck that he had been allotted and once we had exchanged greetings and loaded the back with empty banana boxes and a set of scales we set off. The banana boxes are very sturdy cardboard boxes, made explicitly for transporting bananas (you may have guessed that already) and appear to be the universal receptacle in which to shift supermarket goods and the scales are taken so that FAM can record how much produce has been picked up at each store as that has to be officially recorded and reported back to the appropriate government department.

FAM had five trucks in total, ranging from the largest, which is a GMC 5 tonner, complete with tail-lift to the smallest, which was the two tonne one we were in. All of these have been donated over the years to the organisation by various local companies as they upgrade their fleets and also want to do something to help out a local charity. I'll be very honest in that they weren't kidding when they described ours as 'old'; as it was at least 25 years young and had well over a million miles on the clock, and while it might have huffed and puffed a bit up the hills (well wouldn't you?), it was still going strong. One of the volunteer drivers is a retired mechanic, and so when he's not collecting from supermarkets, he also looks after all the vehicle maintenance. The only real challenge that we found with it was that the passenger door could not be opened from the inside as the door mechanism had given up the ghost a few months previously and the only parts which they could get hold of were for a driver's door, so they had to go with that. It was a bit awkward and involved winding the window down and reaching outside to pull the handle, but once we got the hang of it, we were fine. That said, we kept – fingers well and truly crossed that we wouldn't need to make a hasty exit, which, given the duration of the journeys and speed we were travelling at, was pretty unlikely.

We made four pickups that trip, all at supermarkets and got about half a tonne of produce, mostly foodstuff from fresh fruit and veg, frozen meat through to bread, cakes, biscuits and dairy produce. Some shops pre-sorted the food that they were donating into categories (dairy, meat, grocery, bakery, non-grocery), whilst others would just put it all in boxes and hand it over, so the first job when picking up was to check if it was sorted and if not, that's where the spare banana boxes come in, as we sorted it there and then. This is because it was easier to do at the time, rather than back at the warehouse where it was a little more frantic. The boxes were then duly weighed, the details noted on the clipboard and then we were off to the next place.

The round took about 90 minutes all told and once we had picked up at the final supermarket, we headed back to the warehouse to unload and for Jeff to determine which location to take the food to ('walk-in freezer' for frozen products, 'walk-in fridge' for perishables, 'tables' for wider sorting (cakes, bread, biscuits, cereals, pasta etc.) 'pantry' for food to be distributed that day, or 'Marines van' as Tuesdays and

Fridays are when FAM do a delivery to the US Marines base at Camp Pendleton, just down the road). I did four ride-alongs initially and they were all mostly different routes and shops and with different people, who it was great to meet and talk to.

Trip 1: Total load of half a tonne as above – Doug was a retired engineer who worked at the nuclear power station out near San Onofre beach and which was being decommissioned having got to the end of its 40- or 50-year lifespan. He was a very keen long distance cyclist, who had twice crossed the US from coast to coast, first time was a southerly route from San Diego in California via Texas, Louisiana and the deep south states to Florida, which took two months and the second time more northerly from San Francisco via Salt Lake City, and the mid-west states to New York which was a more 'leisurely' three months. He has also cycled John O'Groats to Lands End, along the back roads of Britain, which took six weeks and another trip was Paris to Istanbul. All in all, a very impressive tally of trips, making me feel positively pedestrian in comparison.

Trip 2: Total load of two tonnes – from larger supermarkets and a longer route, on this occasion I accompanied Dixie. We benefited from Vons supermarket having a large clear out of fresh fruit and veg, which gave us a total of 60 banana boxes of really great apples, tomatoes, berries, etc. Dixie was also retired, he had served for three years in the Marines in Vietnam, before – in his own words – he 'took full advantage of the more liberal lifestyle available to young people at the end of the '60s and early '70s and, to be honest, perhaps a little too much advantage, well at least that is according to my dad, anyway'. What a top bloke! He then ran his own construction business for about 20 years, before a recession hit and he moved to work for the Southern California water company, which is where he spent the last 20 years or so of his working life.

Trip 3: Total load a tonne and a half – this was a slightly shorter route with Samantha and was one where we bagged a lot of ex-Easter and Passover goodies which had gone unsold and included three banana boxes full of Reese's eggs and Cadbury's Creme Eggs. I don't know where you stand on the whole size and taste debate of the Creme Egg, but to me these ones seemed more like the old chunkier size but they tasted the same as in the UK, however that is purely a layman's opinion, as my knowledge of both categories is sketchy, not being a huge consumer. Samantha was a full-time employee at FAM, and usually based at the warehouse, managing the pantry operation, however, when they are short of drivers, she helps out. She had also served in the US forces (army, this time) before having a corporate career with the company who make Doritos where she was VP of the product for a while and so becoming known as Little Miss Dorito. How cool is that? Tiring of the corporate life, she took voluntary redundancy to do stuff at home and then started as a volunteer at FAM about five years ago, before being asked to join the full-time staff after six months.

Trip 4: Total load just over a tonne – this was the shortest route with the four supermarkets closest to the FAM warehouse and was with Doug again. This took in our biggest haul of bakery goods so far, all from Albertson's supermarket, comprising 100 loaves of bread, baguettes, bagels rolls,

doughnuts, pastries, muffins, cream cakes and sundry sticky buns, which despite our valiant efforts, however, some didn't make it back to the warehouse, a few sadly went missing in action…

It was such a lovely, worthwhile and rewarding few weeks with these folks, I didn't have a dull moment, there was always a good laugh to be had and they were extremely welcoming and friendly throughout. It gave me a great insight into how regular people's lives are lived and it enabled me to get in touch with – in a very small way – the 'real' America.

25. Big Bear!
9th May 2019

With Jenny's arrival in California for a week's holiday, we decided to depart the coast for a wee while and go inland, up into the hills for a couple of days. Prior to coming out here, a mate of mine from work called Rob had told me about a resort town about 100 miles from San Clemente called Big Bear, which is renowned for its skiing during the winter and water sports and hiking in the summer, so I had booked us a couple of nights in a hotel in the centre.

The origin of the town name is not clear, some say it's derived from this being 'Big Bear Country', whereas others favour the tale that an early settler arrived back in town one afternoon, very out of breath, white as a sheet, scared witless, bleeding from an obviously violent loss of parts of his scalp and also from scratches sustained by running very quickly through scrub bushes, and when asked what was up, could only gesticulate frantically behind him and say, "Big Bear!!!"

The drive up was very pleasant, as we had decided to take the lesser roads where possible and so hopefully see a little more of small-town America than we would do from the freeways. Thus, as we had left home early, we were able to stop for breakfast on the way at a cracking little diner in Lake Elsinore City called House of Eggs. If you're ever in the area, don't be put off by the odd name and rather unappealing exterior, as this place sold us an Olympic standard breakfast for just $7.99 which had enough food for the both of us.

We cruised over the Santa Ana mountains and down into the fertile valleys, where Big Agriculture thrives – huge cattle ranches and mile upon mile of citrus groves and wineries – all adding their contribution to the wider and very much booming economy of California. Once past all of these, we began to climb steadily up into the mountains, from roughly 1400ft above sea level at Redlands, where we stopped for lunch to topping out at 8400 ft, a few miles outside Big Bear Lake in the space of about 25 miles. There were lots of extraordinary views back down to the valley and of the mountains above and all with a warm sun and cloudless blue sky.

Once in Big Bear and checked into the hotel – called The Big Bear Frontier, very nice room, right by the Lake and priced at a highly competitive $68/night – we thumbed through the various guides and leaflets we had picked up in reception and headed back out of town to walk the Castle Rock Trail. This was a lovely 90-minute round trip walk up a gulley and through the woods above the town to the top of an escarpment with 360-degree panoramic views of the lake, town and surrounding area. Whether we actually got to the Castle Rock itself, we were not sure there were two or three possibilities to choose from, but as the vistas from our spot were superb. it didn't really seem to matter if we had actually made it to the top.

The following day we got up relatively early for a stroll along Lakeshore Drive, before we headed along the road to Baldwin Stables, where we had booked a two-hour horse ride. Overnight the temperature had dropped significantly from around 20 Celsius to about four and so in addition to the essential long trousers, we had donned fleeces, coats and gloves, all items of clothing which hitherto I had not needed to wear out here. On arrival at the stables, we had to sign the obligatory consent and liability waiver forms, before our allocated gee gees were brought out; I was given Barnaby and Jenny was given Maverick – I didn't ask if 'Goose', was available as we all know what happened to him when the pair went into a tailspin…

The ride was along bridle paths and through scrub pine forest, which, quite uniquely, is also home to cacti and Joshua trees and then wound its way up to the top of a nearby mountain for the touristy snaps of us and our trusty steeds, looking fully at home in this classic western environment. Part of the route we were on follows some of the Pacific Crest Trail, which is a 2500-mile long-distance hiking path from Mexico to the Canadian border – film fans may recognise the name from the Reece Witherspoon movie 'Wild' from a few years ago. It was enormous fun and our guide Tracy was very informative and helpful and ensured we made it up and back without mishap.

That said, by the time we returned to the stables, we were very cold as the weather had started closing in, so we headed back towards Big Bear Lake, pausing for lunch at the Broadway café, where we had chicken tortilla soup to warm up – the chicken being in the soup and the broken up bits of tortilla being on the side, along with grated cheese for us to add to choice. If it sounds bizarre, well, it was a bit, but it actually worked really rather well and given how hungry and cold we were, it was very welcome.

There then followed a quiet afternoon of TV watching and warming back up in the room and in the evening a superb Nepalese curry at the Himalayan restaurant in town. If you have the time, I thoroughly recommend a visit to Big Bear Lake for the walks, the fresh air, the good food and the wonderful peace and quiet away from the hustle and bustle of the coast.

26. Night Life
13th May 2019

Hands up anyone who likes the words 'Happy' and 'Hour' when used together? Most of you? Good, I'm clearly in touch with the right demographic then. Well, in San Clemente (and no doubt elsewhere in California), it was taken very seriously and was rarely just an hour. Most of the bars and restaurants have a good selection of beers, wines and cocktails, as well as food and at roughly half price between 4 pm and 7 pm on Mondays through Fridays. I also found that if I was canny with it, I could rock up at 6:45 pm, order a double round of drinks, get my food order in quickly and was then able to make a really good start to the night and at the same time taking care of my wallet.

Iva Lee's was quite a regular haunt for me as it was only five-minute-walk from my apartment and they had live music Friday/Saturday/Sunday. One memorable night, I saw a group called Finger Fungus (yes, I agree, they could do with some finessing of their name), who were a really great three-piece band. They played excellent covers of songs by artists as diverse as Prince, Tom Petty, Blur, Beatles, Stones, Credence, Roxy Music, Killers and (ahem) Sheryl Crowe. With a new name and some of their own material, I could see those guys going a long way – they can't have been much over 21 or so – much later on in the evening and after several pitchers of beer I was actively considering a late career change into band management; however as that was after I had also considered a career change into setting up a micro-brewery and chop-house with a couple of people I had got talking to in the bar it was unlikely to come to fruition. Another couple of bars which were much on my itinerary were Mulligans and Beachfire – the former with six pool tables and the latter with a great deal of surf memorabilia on the walls. Both were sports bars with an extensive list of beers, thus enabling me to maintain my fledgling interest in baseball, while doing my best to sample as much of the local beer scene.

Speaking of which, over the last ten years or so there has been a significant renaissance of brewing culture in the US – much like the UK, I guess. As I remember it, the first time I went out to the states in the '90s, all that was generally available was the generic fizzy pish from Bud, Coors, Miller, etc. but now most of the towns I have visited have at least one local brewery, if not two, and manage to produce some really great beers. There are a lot of IPAs (India Pale Ale) brewed, most of which are stronger than those produced in Britain (6 to 9% is often the norm) so I quickly learnt to exercise a bit of caution when at the bar as my initial approach of, 'Hmm, 8% eh? That sounds a good place to start,' lead in the first couple of weeks to much earlier ends to evenings than had been planned (and yes, you're quite right, perhaps I ought to have learnt by now, but some things seem to be just unlearnable…).

The bars I visited were all welcoming and I always found folk to chat to at the bar – I'm not trying to make out everywhere was like Cheers, but folk did genuinely strike up conversations and were interested in who I was, why I was there, etc. I never had the experience where on walking into a place, the music would stop and everyone would stare at me, but on just a couple of occasions, I did feel the need to order quickly, down my drink at pace and make a speedy exit.

The first time this happened, was early on in the trip when I walked into Iva Lee's and found that that night, I was the youngest person there (yes, you did read that correctly) and by about 20 years. It turned out they were having a senior citizen date reunion night and when I went back a couple of nights later, normal service and regular clientele were restored. The second occasion was the polar opposite and happened in Mulligans, when it was clearly goth night and as

I'd omitted to bring any black clothes or eyeshadow, my baggy shorts and surf tee-shirt didn't really cut the mustard, so again, I beat a hasty retreat. It's not that I had anything against any of the people on either occasion, but when having a pint, I do like to feel like I'm fitting in at least a bit…

27. Out and About Again
16th May 2019

During the course of my trip I made quite an effort to make my time away a little less one dimensional and so I tried to get myself out a fair amount to enjoy a good slice of non-surf-related activities, after all, there's no point paying for the full buffet and only going for mac and cheese...

O'Neil Regional Park

One such example was after our return from Big Bear, Jenny and I took ourselves off to O'Neil Regional park, which is about 20 minutes away in the hills above San Clemente. It's managed by the Orange County authorities and is an area of 'designated wilderness', which means that it is protected from development and is maintained for the benefit of both people who wish to enjoy it as well as the wildlife who call it home. The park has a number of well-marked out paths for hiking, biking and horse riding, and it's highly recommended that folk keep to these, as there is an abundance of local wild critters, who, if disturbed, would leave you wishing you'd been a tad more respectful of their space (e.g. coyote, bobcats, rattlers and mountain lions).

Fortunately for us, we didn't have any unplanned beasty incidents, because in most cases, they will hear you coming a long time before you become aware of them and they scarper pretty rapidly. It's a lovely peaceful park, which, given its close proximity to the million or so people who live within 30 minutes' drive of it, is really quite remarkable – definitely a good one to visit again.

On another occasions, when I was parking at Doheny Beach for an early morning ride, I found much of the car park was cordoned off, but with no obvious sign of a reason why, however as I was there for waves, I put it from my mind and headed out. On returning a couple of hours later, all was revealed, for that day was the annual 'Doheny Woodie Show' – yes, yes, I know, it made me snigger too. However, this wasn't the annual contest to find Orange County's proudest member (hopefully that would be held somewhere a little more private, although 'held' is possibly not the best choice of word either), but it was, in fact, a vintage car show, and specifically cars with wooden frames and side panels.

Now I'm not really a car buff – to which anyone who's familiar with my choice in vehicles will testify – however, I couldn't fail to be impressed with what was on show, as it was a huge collection of around 100 makes and models. This included some from the '20s and '30s, as well as many from the post WWII golden years of American car manufacturing, featuring a number of makes that no longer exist – Oldsmobile, Mercury, Plymouth, Studebaker – and there were even a few of Oxford's finest Morris Minors on show; although in all honesty, these did look like Matchbox cars when parked alongside the behemoths that the Detroit companies produced. The vast majority had been beautifully restored and very well maintained, whilst a few were works in progress, but with proud owners all of them. It was quite some spectacle.

28. Giving a Little Back, Part III
20th May 2019

As my time in San Clemente was drawing to a close (eight weeks had never passed so quickly) I continued to help out with FAM and whilst Jenny was staying, she also joined in the fun, and to make it even more special, I was given the keys to Old Betsy to drive, and so the two of us went out on a food pick-up round on our own. Now, Old Betsy is roughly the size of a Luton box van, which I've driven before when moving house, however, I've not driven anything of this size, or venerability in the States, so I was a little cautious to start with. Once we got going, though, it was a blast – sure, she rattled and creaked and struggled a bit and so what if the doors didn't open too easily, but let's be honest as she had done two and quarter million miles to date, I would say that she's fully entitled to a bit of huff and puff, wouldn't you? In terms of food collected, we got a decent haul of about a ton of mixed produce from three supermarkets, before heading back to unload and then fill one of the other vans for the twice weekly drop off at Camp Pendleton.

In my final week I did a few pickups, including two and half tons of food from five supermarkets with Robert on Monday. This was quite a longish route, where we covered about 60 miles all told. The reason there was more on this round than usual, was that the previous day had been US Mother's Day , so there was a great deal of unsold party food – cakes, bread, and buffet items, etc. Robert and I had plenty of good chat to accompany the drive, and I discovered that he was a retired investment manager who had grown up in Minnesota in the Midwest, where seasonal temperatures are at the real extremes (winters can be as cold as -40 Celsius and summers as hot at +35), so a strong constitution and a lot of perseverance are required to survive. He had been in California for about 20 years now, and unsurprisingly had no desire to move back – but he does visit from time to time.

On my final day helping out I was asked to do a round on my own in 'Little Yellow' which is their two-ton truck. I picked up just over a ton of mostly bread, cakes and sticky buns from a couple of Ralph's supermarkets, all again left over from the weekend. The truck was as easy to drive as a regular car and it was great to be asked to help out in that way. Once I'd finished the round and unloaded, I went into the office to say my goodbyes to the people I had got to know over the last few weeks, and to my surprise, they had convened a staff meeting to present me with a Certificate of Appreciation for the work I'd done. I was really touched by this as it was a great privilege to be able to get involved and help out at FAM. who right from the outset, were all very welcoming and went out of their way to make me feel part of the team. My memories of my time there still stay with me.

29. So, Do I Cut the Mustard?
21st May 2019

Once I reached the end of the San Clemente part of my trip, this concluded the end of the focus on surfing and so I felt it was time for a reckoning on how I had progressed and how 'good' I had become. The final few weeks were all at either Doheny and Oceanside beaches and I made a great deal of use of both the soft-top eight ft board and the 6'6" shortboard to practice and hone my skills. I greatly enjoyed using the latter, and was able to catch and ride some waves bigger than before, as well as do some good turns and fast moves. However, as I previously reported, the shortboard was a lot more unpredictable and pernickety to use, and as the waves were not often of the right size and power, I was not able to perfect it as much as I would have liked; whilst I may have been rather disappointed about this, there was not a lot I could do to change it.

My surfing knowledge had increased hugely – for instance, I learnt a vast amount about wave formation, how to anticipate them and read how they would behave. I now knew about the different types of break and how they can be approached, as well as how to be confident of looking at incoming surf on a beach, and knowing whether or not I would be able to get out and ride or whether I'd be better off chilling until the risk to life/limb is reduced.

So, the final reckoning …

Ability: I had made really big improvements all round, my wave selection whilst not 100%, was easily in the 70 to 80% range and my ride rate was certainly above 50%.

Technique: My pop-up had become very clean, with my feet landing in the right place 90% of the time, there was still an occasional miss, wobble and being dumped in the ocean, for sure, but they had become much rarer. My paddling – both out to the line-up and to catch a wave – was much stronger, granted it would still take up a great deal of energy, but that's the same for everyone and I was way less knackered than I used to be once I got outside the breaking water.

Style: Hmmm, yeah, OK; I have to admit, this was never going to be my strong suit, but I was looking less like a puppet on a string than I used to and I was much quicker to address any unbalancing – not that I always stayed on, obviously…Aside from that, though, I had taught myself to cross step to the nose of the board and back without tipping off (i.e. walk the length of the board and back), but the fabled 'hang ten' movement (where you stand still on the nose of the board with all ten toes hanging off the end) was not yet in my grasp. One to aim for, I think.

Approach: My confidence was much better with the larger waves, I might not always have caught them, but then, I wouldn't really have expected to quite yet – the main thing was that I was happy to go for them.

Enthusiasm: Boom! Oh Yeah! Still got bags and bags of this and in all honesty, this is never likely to dip below the 'Bring it on!' level.

Best Day: I caught six waves on the bounce, each one was a majestic line of unbroken water, ridden for between 50 and 80 meters each – for which I even got a, 'Woah, sweeeeet ride, dude!' from a gal in the line-up when paddled back out. Yeah, I'll not deny it, that did feel good.

Grade: A-

There was still room for improvement, especially with the shortboard and some of the main tricks and skills, but from the standing start of eight weeks previously, I was unrecognisable. I was very, very pleased.

For my last week in San Clemente I was joined by Evie and the two of us went out a few times and caught some excellent video footage including as absolute cracker on my last day on the water, where we caught the same wave and rode it in together. That was very cool.

Evie had joined me, obviously for some surfing, but the main event for her visit was just about to start, as the two of us were about to set off on a road trip from Orange County all the way up the coast to the top of California and into Oregon, then back down the middle and far side of the state, before we were to finish up in San Francisco.

30. King of the Road
23rd May 2019

One major aspect of my visit was the amount of time I had spent in the car and over the course of the eight weeks I had been out, I had clocked up just over 3,200 miles on the roads, and generally, I would say it was a pretty stress-free experience. Whilst in San Clemente, I had been driving a Toyota Highlander SUV which was very good as it ticked the primary box, namely, shed-loads of space to comfortably accommodate surfboards, people, luggage, my ego, etc. definitely the right choice for what I needed…

I found public transport in the area to be very limited, compared to the UK (e.g. there was a single track rail line between San Diego and LA, which offered only an infrequent and slow service, and whilst there were buses, they only supported local municipalities), so the main way to really get about was via car, which consequently meant that the volume of traffic was colossal. Major travel of any distance was always via the freeways and the ones between here and LA and San Diego were just enormous. They were all at least five lanes in each direction and in many cases seven or eight and seemingly at all times during the day they were chocker – I didn't go out at night much admittedly, so couldn't comment on that, but from 6 am to 10 pm, they were full. A recent addition to the freeways had been the carpool lanes for vehicles with two or more people in them, and so I was able to use these a fair bit when I had people staying, but car was very much king here as the overwhelming majority of folk travel on their own – be it to work or to the shops.

I was very impressed with how people drove. As you would expect, there were the usual loopers, who weaved in and out of traffic at high speed – but let's be honest, you get those muppets everywhere. In the main, folk were very considerate on the road, e.g. if I happened to be in the wrong lane, people would let me move across without trying to block me, and I never came come across any examples of road rage or drivers being cut up or had anyone flip the international digit of disdain. I rarely heard horns going off either, and as a bonus, there were no middle-lane pootlers, who would refuse to pull over and therefore slowed everyone else down (that said, this was probably because there were many more lanes to choose from).

However, the two most noticeable things were:

1. Everyone drove either at or above the speed limit, on the freeways, where 65 mph was generally the limit, there was hardly anyone below that, and this included trucks and 90% of folk drove at 75 or more.
2. Overtaking on the inside was a regular and legal approach to going passed other cars. At first, I found doing this a little disconcerting as it went against everything I had ever been taught and told in the UK; however, given the size of the roads and amount of traffic, provided it was done safely and sensibly, it actually worked really well, as it stopped traffic bunching on the inside lanes and reduced driver

frustration, as they would decide for themselves when and how they should pass other vehicles, rather than being reliant on someone else to move over. It may not be to everyone's taste and it wouldn't work everywhere, but for me, I certainly did not think it was the devil that it's often made out to be.

Similarly, the condition of the roads I found to be also very good; the freeways were in the main concrete and well maintained, and the ordinary town and country roads usually tarmac, and in most cases, mill-pond smooth, which made for very comfortable driving. I certainly found this going up into the mountains to Big Bear, where a lot of care was clearly taken to ensure the roads were in good nick, as the contrasts between winter and summer conditions are stark and must play havoc with the surfaces.

I would shortly find out if this idyll would be constant throughout the state and beyond, as our grand road trip was about to be begin and for this, we had hired a Jeep Wrangler – oooh, can you feel that American Dream…?

31. Coast Roads, Part I
27th May 2019

Big Sur

If you like driving and you're a fan of coast roads, then California Highway 1 is a must. The road itself runs the full length of the state, but the part that most people wish to see is located on the central coast between San Luis Obispo and Carmel and offers a stretch of about 130 winding miles of coastline hugging nirvana. For travellers doing the south to north route, San Luis Obispo is about 180 miles north of LA and then Carmel is 120 miles south of San Francisco.

It is by far the most dramatic stretch of road I've ever driven on – with the mountains of Pfeiffer State Park looming up on one side and sheer 400 ft drops to the ocean on the other, it really is jaw-droppingly astonishing. There are rocky outcrops like dragon's teeth, standing sentinel all along the coast, which are relentlessly pounded by the surge and might of the Pacific and around each bend, there are new vistas and heart-stoppingly precipitous cliffs, no two views are the same.

Towards the top of the road (which was the north end as we were travelling south to north), we arrived at the Bixby Creek Bridge, which, in itself, is an eye-catching sight. It was built in 1932 and to this day, it remains the longest single span concrete arch bridge anywhere in the world. The road is well maintained throughout, which, given the extremes of weather ocean and annual rock falls it endures, is no mean feat. We took our leisurely time on the road as there were plenty of stopping points and laybys enabling us to pause and admire the view, and despite the number of tourists who were on it, it did not feel at all crowded.

Pacific Grove and 17 Mile Drive

We stopped overnight in a town just north of Carmel called Pacific Grove which has another scenic road winding along and around the Monterey Peninsula called 17 Mile Drive. This part of the coast is owned and run as a designated state park and includes Pebble Beach golf course, which to an American golfer this place has the same resonance as that which St Andrews has to a British one. The coastline is similar to Big Sur in that it is very rugged and dramatic, but with the difference that it can be enjoyed at ground level either on foot or on a bike, which gave it, for us, an altogether different and much closer perspective.

We hired bikes for the day so that we could take it all fully in and also so that we could get out of the car for a while, and as the wind was blowing a fair old hooley, we decided to go for fat-tyre electric bikes. These were great fun, and work on the principle that the motor kicks in when you pedal and the more you pedal, the more the motor works They also had throttles for extra bursts of speed, and which were perfect for us both into wind and/or going uphill.

Unusually for an American road, it had been built with bikes in mind, and so there was plenty of room for us and the cars, buses, etc. so there was no feeling of being hemmed in or at risk. Along the way, we went through the woods, filled with cypress trees and passed coves, cliffs, bluffs, white sand beaches, and we also saw the lone cypress tree, which is used as the image and logo of Pebble Beach – similar to the bridge over the Swilken Burn at St Andrews. It was a very satisfying

– and tiring – day, but as a way of seeing one of California's most iconic places, I don't think a bike could have beaten it.

32. Coast Roads, Part II
28th May 2019

The North Coast

Leaving the Monterey Peninsula and Pebble Beach, we headed north around the great sweep of Monterey Bay, past the welcoming dunes of Sand City and the chilled seaside city of Santa Cruz, where wooden roller coasters still run at the amusement park, surfers flock to the never-ending breaks and '60s/'70s' dropouts can still be found hiding from Nixon, the Vietnam draft and pretty much everything else which has happened since that first tab of acid brought about their paranoia (NB for movie fans, Santa Cruz was the setting for the '80s' vampire flick *The Lost Boys…*).

The roads were pretty quiet until we got close to San Francisco, but as this was just a passing visit, we pushed on through and out of the city, then over the Golden Gate Bridge. I expect that most people are aware, but this really is quite a structure, built in the 1930s over the Bay Strait, linking San Francisco to Marin County, it was for some time the longest suspension bridge in the world. To this day it continues to carry three lanes of traffic in each direction and thereby showing that in the early 20th century politicians were unable to design and build a bridge to cope with future traffic capacity; which, puts it in sharp contrast to the folk who commissioned the recently opened New Forth Road Bridge, which is already maxed out at rush hour – but that's enough about the incompetence of bureaucrats and politicians.

Being one of the most iconic bridges in the world, it was great to drive across and add to the road trip memory canon. We cruised up the 101 freeway for 30 miles or so, before cutting across country to re-join Highway 1 at Bodega Bay, which we then followed for around 180 miles up to Fort Bragg. This is another very scenic stretch of coast, and although it's significantly less rugged than Big Sur, it's no less dramatic – tree-lined mountains and grass-covered hills roll more gently down to the shoreline, where it joins with more rocks, reefs and skerries in the booming surf.

The Lost Coast

Heading out the next day from Fort Bragg, Highway 1 took us up the coast again for a short distance, before turning

inland and into the forests of the Coastal Redwoods. After a couple of hours or so meandering through groves of the tallest trees imaginable, we came to a turning signposted for Cape Mendocino. I had read about this in one of the guidebooks, as this is where California's most westerly point is located and this particular stretch is what's known as The Lost Coast. It gets this name because of its inaccessibility, as the winding road to it from the forest traverses the tops of two mountains and the one leading back to the town of Eureka and civilisation crosses yet another mountain and an expanse of bleak, windswept moor. This might have put off other less doughty travellers, but to us, it sounded an ideal place to put the Jeep Wrangler through its paces, so off we headed.

The ascent of the first mountain was not bad as the road climbed from about 200 feet above sea level to 3000 feet in a little under five miles or so, and apart from a few potholes, it was pretty smooth going and the view from the top down the valley and over the far countryside was stunning and we had it all to ourselves – or so we thought. As once we at the summit, we had parked up and were sat atop the Wrangler to admire the view when from round a bend three cyclists arrived from the other direction and not looking too stressed about the ascent they had just made. We chatted to them for a while and they told us they were members of a cycling club from Eureka and this route was a regular weekender for getting themselves into shape. We were certainly impressed and became even more so on the route down, as this was a lot trickier, because there had recently been a few rockfalls which had narrowed the road, leaving quite a lot of debris in their wake, but by using some astute steering and braking ensured we got down safely.

The second mountain, however, was a whole different ballgame – many stretches of the road were just dirt and gravel track, in four or five places landslides had halved the width of the road, with only a couple of traffic cones marking the danger spots and there were plenty of places where the angle of ascent/descent were so steep it felt that sliding would be inevitable. However, after 90 heart-pumping minutes, we reached the coast and what a sight it was – a 10 mile stretch with the road at sea level, cliffs and mountains, rearing up on the one side, and on the other, a shoreline so peppered with boulders, sharply angled rocks and long jagged reefs that there was barely any beach to be seen. Truly extraordinary. To cap the surreal feeling of it all, a sign told us there was a layby a half mile or so up the road and so we decided we would pull in to take in the view. However, when we got there, we found it already occupied by a guy in a convertible, sitting in the driving seat with the door open playing his saxophone. We could have stopped and watched him, but we felt that as he had made the effort to drive to one of the most remote parts of the state for a jam, the last thing he would actually want was an audience.

After that, the drive back out offered yet more sections of steep hairpin bends, eyebrow-raising drops to valley floors, and at one point on the moor, in rolled the fog to envelope us in its thick wet blanket, which billowed all around us, reducing visibility to 20 feet or so – seriously atmospheric. In total, it took about four hours to do the 50 or so miles, which I'll admit is a long time, but it was absolutely worth the effort and as for the Wrangler – not a grumble. The engine temperature increased barely a jot, the cooler fans hardly kicked in and the acceleration and brakes were never less than superb, all in a day's work. Full marks to Jeep from us.

33. Amongst the Giants
31st May 2019

Leaving Fort Bragg, we headed inland and into the Redwood forests of the coastal mountain ranges, the roads started to wind a bit more, the inclines became a bit steeper, the roadside foliage was denser and the sunlight much reduced. We were now in the Land of The Giants…

The Giant Redwood is a tree from the Sequoia Sempervirens species and it differs from the Giant Sequoia (Sequoiadendron giganteum – of which, much more in a later chapter) in that its natural habitat is within five to 20 miles of the Northern California Coast, where the annual temperature, level of rainfall and altitude of between 500 and 4000 feet provides them with the ideal growing environment. The average lifespan is 1,800 years and average height is 350 feet (90 m) with the oldest known to be 2,500 years (not long after Rome was founded) and the tallest reaching 397 ft (115 m); which is taller than Big Ben and only a smidgeon shorter than the London Eye, making them by some way the tallest and amongst the oldest living things on the planet.

Our first forest stop was the Drive Thru' – a phrase which often precedes misunderstood orders, cold food, lingering odours in the car and general disappointment all round. However, on this occasion, there was not a microphone interface or burger in sight and plenty of fun to be had as we had come across the fabled Tree You Can Drive Through!

I had read about this as a child and had been fascinated by the thought as where I grew up trees were big and tall (as a child most things are bigger and taller), but not exceptionally so and certainly not of the size where a car could be driven through, so this was a real treat. This particular Giant Redwood had been caught in a forest fire in the mid to late 19th century and consequently a hole had burnt right the way through part of the base of its trunk. Now whereas for most trees that sort of damage would mean it would die, this is not usually the case with Sequoias as fire has always been a natural forest occurrence and they have evolved to have natural defences against it which enable them to survive burnings and having chunks missing from them. In this instance the enterprising land-owner had realised the hole was big enough for people to walk through several abreast and so it was not a lot of work to widen the hole and put a track through it so that cars could drive through. And so, that's what we did and the Drive Thru' has never held the same meaning since.

Our tree-tunnel appetites sated, we then moved on up the freeway and came off at Humboldt Redwood State Park, where there is a 30 mile stretch of road which follows the meandering course of the Eel River through the park and is called the Avenue of the Giants. Coming across the first parking area, we got out and wandered along a looping trail, passing so many colossal trees that we quickly lost count and just stared in awe at what we could see. Everywhere we looked, it seemed as though there were trees bigger than the last ones spotted. We did a crude measurement around the base of one particular giant by counting the number of arm-spans it took to make it round – which gave us an astonishing figure of 25m. Now that's a big tree...

Trees which had fallen to the ground were as fascinating as the ones still alive, as we could stand in the shadow of the roots – often seven or eight metres in diameter and we could also walk along the length of the intact trunks, most of which were 70 to 80 meters before we came to the top sections, which had snapped off when falling. We spoke to one ranger who told us that the noise and reverberation when one of these giants fall, is not dis-similar to a bomb going off, such is the effect.

We spent two full days, hiking and horse-riding through the forests, and in addition to the trees, we came across elk, fresh bear tracks and innumerable bird species – although we could hear no birdsong down on the ground, which we put down to the fact that the tree canopy is so far above that the sounds do not come down that far. We did see some bears when out on the horse ride, but as they were about a quarter of a mile away, we were not close enough to know whether they were brown, black or grizzly – which is probably not a bad thing.

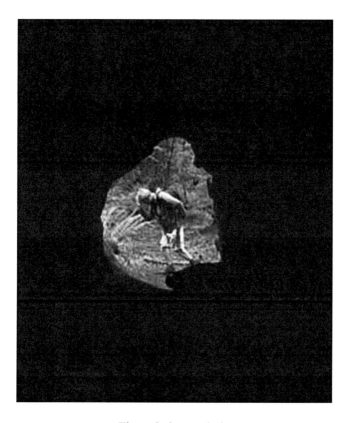

Through the tree hole

34. Mountains and Lakes, Part I
2nd June 2019

Leaving Giant Redwood country, we drove inland, following the Rogue River out of California and up into the mountains of Southern Oregon, where our next stop was Crater Lake National Park. Arriving there in the late afternoon, we stopped off at the visitor centre to find out all we could.

Crater Lake is what remains of a volcano called Mount Mazama, which erupted about 7,700 years ago. Over the preceding half a million years, the mountain had been slowly growing via a series of eruptions and had reached a height of circa 14,500 feet, which is when it really started to blow. Accounts from the local Native American tribe recorded at the time show that over the course of about a week, it spewed so much rock, ash and other debris, it managed to cover an area of 10,000 square miles in said rock, ash etc. to an average depth of two feet.

Once this had finished, there was a period of a few days when all was quiet, but this was then broken one morning by another series of huge explosions, which lasted several hours and turned out to be the cone of the mountain collapsing in on itself. The result of which was a huge circular crater five miles by six miles across and an average of 3,500 feet deep. Further to that, the scale of the eruption and subsequent collapse had reduced the mountain's height by half to an average of 7,500 feet – it had quite literally blown its top off.

With the crater now formed, the mountain was quiet for the next 300 years or so, before a series of new eruptions occurred, some of which were large enough to create new peaks within the crater – the largest being Wizard Peak, which can still be seen in the middle of the crater and has the classic volcano shape…

Over the course of the of the next 3000 years, it began to fill with water from the annual rainfall and snowmelt, slowly filling it to the level it remains at to this day. If you think that sounds unlikely, I should add that the Crater Lake area is also the snowiest place in America as it receives on average 44ft of snow every year. That is a lot of snow. The average depth of the lake is 1,148 feet and its lowest point of 1,949 feet also makes it the deepest lake in North America. The water level remains pretty much constant due to natural evaporation and seepage through the porous rocks at circa 5,000ft and despite the intense winter cold its five trillion gallons of water, which circulates up and down, ensures that it never freezes over.

The snow usually starts to fall in mid-September with the last seasonal falls during May (in fact, it had snowed just two days before we arrived), and it will often still be lying on the ground well into July, which is why when we were there we found ourselves dwarfed by the huge drifts even with a daytime temperature of 12 degrees.

Incidentally, it is a 'trapped' lake, i.e. one which has no inbound or outbound streams, there are no naturally occurring fish or other water creatures in it; however in the early 20th century a resident or pioneer, I forget which did introduce 15 or 20 trout to the lake and so their ancestors continue to thrive, but not in huge numbers.

It's an extraordinary place of ethereal beauty, with the water acting as a mirror for the crater rim, cliff faces and sky, and the water is so clear that the naked eye can see objects 140 ft below the surface. A true place of wonder and awe.

35. Mountains and Lakes, Part II
3rd June 2019

Having drunk our fill of Crater Lake, as it were, we moved on and back down into California to our next stop – Lake Tahoe. However, before us was a not insubstantial 400-mile drive and with none of that on freeways, we would have to take ordinary highways and back roads up and over the mountain passes. So, we got ourselves up just as dawn was breaking and were packed and out of the door by 5am, with plans for a hearty breakfast a stop along the way.

Driving at that time was a real treat as the roads were clear and with the sun was coming up, illuminating the snow-covered mountains, before it rose further to fill the valleys with light. We made extremely good progress, and after an hour and a half or so, having passed the towering slopes of Mount Shasta, a 14,200ft dormant volcano, we arrived in the wonderfully named town of Weed.

Having thought ahead, Google found us a well-reviewed diner on the main street called The Hi-Lo Café, and it was indeed superb – standing-ovation-level eggs benedict, followed by we-are-not-worthy waffles, syrup and fruit. The experience was further enhanced by us being seated behind the local sheriff, who was discussing prospects for the candidates to succeed him in the upcoming election; it couldn't have been more Dukes of Hazard if we'd been talking to Boss Hogg.

Breakfast done, we headed into the Weed tourist shop and bought as much town-branded merchandise as our credit cards would allow us (well, c'mon, how often were we going to be able to buy a legit 'Weed Rocks' t-shirt…?).

We then decided to take the road to Lake Tahoe via Lassen Volcanic National Park, which would have been a peach of a route, winding up and around the 10,500 ft Lassen Peak, which last erupted just over 100 years ago. However, once we got there, we found that the route through the park was closed due to heavy snow, so instead, we satisfied ourselves with climbing over the lava fields left from the previous eruption, before hitting the road again.

10 minutes back down the road and we were glad not to be outside as the sky had gone black, thunder and lightning were going off all around us, the temperature had dropped from 22 degrees Celsius to five, and we were being battered from above by hailstones the size of large marbles. 20 minutes beyond that, we were down in the valley, the sky had cleared, the sun was out and the temperature was back up at 25 degrees Celsius – you could say that the weather is kind of changeable here...

And so, we headed on, pestered by an occasional monsoon downpour, which rudely shoved aside Mr Sun and his hat, before finally arriving in South Lake Tahoe at just after 6 pm, 13 hours after we set off, tired, relieved and just a little frazzled. Some days are just like that, I guess...

36. Mountains and Lakes, Part III
5th June 2019

Waking up to sunlight streaming through the curtains and the sound of waves lapping gently nearby could only mean one thing, we were on the shores of Lake Tahoe and what a place it is…

It is a glacial lake, 20 miles long, by 12 wide and with its ski slopes (the lake is high up in the Sierra Nevada mountains), 70 miles of shoreline, 300+ days per year of sunshine and famed casinos, the towns surrounding Lake Tahoe have long been playgrounds for those looking for a place to relax and unwind. It is situated on the eastern side of the state and in fact a good third of the lake's eastern shoreline is in Nevada as the state line passes through the middle of the lake.

Having spent most of the previous day in the car, we were in dire need of fresh air and exercise, so we headed to the Eagle Falls trail and set off up the mountain. This was a very popular route to hike, with a very well defined path which led up to a good viewing spot, after which most folk seemed to decide to head back down to their cars, however, as this had only taken us about 20 minutes, our walking and fresh air needs had barely been touched.

We knew what we needed – ideally, a route where we would have to use our heads to think about which rocks to step on, one where we could use our hands to grip, while swinging our feet to the next ledge, something to get the heart pumping and the adrenaline flowing – what we needed was a cliff-face scramble.

We looked about us and there was a peak about 600 feet above, which was a combination of boulder, scrubland, cliff and rocky incline – and it looked perfect. So off we went, one of us with cat-like grace and agility, while the other rather less feline and a bit more bovine. It took us about an hour of good climbing and occasional head-scratching of the "Hmm, yes, now we have got to this part, I can see you were right and we can go no further, sorry about that Evie" type. But eventually once we reached the top the reward was worth it, as the view was superb and it was ours and ours alone to enjoy.

For our second day at Tahoe, we wanted to enjoy its key feature – i.e. the lake – and having rifled through the various tourist leaflets and other bumf, advertising boat trips, paddle boarding, water-skiing, etc. we set upon kayaking as the perfect activity as we'd both done it before, we could do it together and it was unlikely we would end up stranded miles from where we started. So off we went around to Emerald Bay, paid our money, put on the lifejackets, and after a quick safety chat, climbed in and paddled off.

The bay is a three-mile-long inlet on the south western shore and gets its name from the reflections of the pine trees on the hillsides all around. To begin with, we paddled over to an island in the middle of the bay and climbed to a building at its top which is called the Tea House. It was so-called as an early 20th century owner of the bay and surrounding land used to have herself rowed out to it by her resident hermit in order to take tea there. Actually, being a hermit (hermiting or hermitery?) was really only a part-time gig for him, as he was also employed as the caretaker for her big house on the lakeshore when she was away and only decamped to the island when she was in residence.

The kayaking was great fun as we got to explore the shoreline from a different perspective, the clear waters meant we could see far below the surface to the plants and rocks on the bottom – however, as there weren't any fish we could see, we had to leave our angling ambitions and thoughts of catching something for dinner on hold.

Returning the kayak on time and with no wobbly mishaps, we drove round to the north eastern corner of the lake to Incline Village, where we had heard that a lakeshore path had been recently opened. Driving into a car park by the lake and pausing by the booth to enquire how much it would cost to park and walk the path, we unfortunately encountered one of those ladies of the twin-set and pearls, snooty-boots brigade for whom the power to allow/refuse access had clearly gone to her head – I was pretty certain that had we looked closely, she would have had a peaked cap, trench coat and jackboots hidden under the counter.

Anyway, in a manner best described as 'brusque yet patronising', she informed us, 'This beachfront is for Village residents only,' which, OK that is fair enough, I can understand that, this is a popular spot and restricting access to locals only can be done, if that's what they want.

However, to my question, 'Do you know where we can park to access the lakeshore path?' she threw me a look as though I'd picked up her coffee, lifted the lid a touch and belched into it before handing it back and then simply parroted her 'This beachfront is for Village residents only' mantra.

She then pointed and added – with just a little bit too much emphasis on the first word – 'YOU will need to go three miles that way if YOU want to go on the beach.'

At this point, I was tempted to say, 'So you can only come here if you're one of the Village People then?' but I rather suspected that her knowledge of '70s' LBGT disco heroes would be limited and my crack would fall flat – if you'll pardon the expression.

Anyway, undeterred, we moved on round the lake to Sandy Harbour, which is at the other end of the lakeshore path and walked there instead. What a joy it was, it offered uninterrupted views across the lake to the mountains of the High Sierra, brand new bridges over creeks and inlets allowing us to look into the clear deep waters and all the time accompanied by the scents from the native plants and bushes lining the route. Very tranquil and the perfect antidote to being in the car, so good in fact we celebrated our walk with ice lollies and a paddle in the cool lake waters. Marvellous. As lakes for leisure go, Tahoe takes some beating.

37. Trees That Please, Part I
8th June 2019

An early alarm call could only mean one thing – it was a hit the road day again. This time it was a slightly shorter 340 miles and a rather more straightforward route down the freeway. We had considered taking a more scenic route through Yosemite National Park, which would have been a similar distance, but would have added about four hours to the journey time. However, as it happened, that option was not available as the road was still blocked by the winter snow – the Park's highest elevation is about 9,500 feet and it was not expected to be open until the end of June.

We made our way away from Lake Tahoe and headed down the mountain passes to the freeways in the valley below. Driving through the city of Folsom, we looked for the prison so we could sing along to Jonny Cash's blues classic, but perhaps for that very reason, the road does not go past it. By lunchtime, we were through Fresno and on the road to Giant Sequoia National Park – for me, there was a great sense of anticipation growing, as this has long been my favourite of the parks and I was hoping that it would not disappoint.

On the freeway in the valley, the temperature was in the high 20s degrees Celsius, but it started to drop as we steadily began to climb into the mountains again. As a rule of thumb, the temperature will drop by an average of a couple of degrees or so for every 1000 feet you ascend, so by the time we got to the park entrance at 5000 feet, it was down to a much more comfortable 18. Unfortunately, it proceeded to drop further as the sky also darkened dramatically, and by the time we reached the Grant Village visitor centre, it was down to eight and we were in a repeat cycle of the monster hail we had had at Lassen. We did begin to wonder if this was a National Park special, put on just for us.

Fortunately, it was short lived and having holed up in the Park Visitor Centre where we picked up trial maps and helpful leaflets with instructions on how to deal with bears which approach: either (a) run at them, making as much noise as possible (aye, right. OK, you go first eh? Or (b) if it's a grizzly, lie on the ground and pretend to be dead (hmm, right, as if a grizzly sniffing you isn't going to lead to an unwanted escape of noise or other excretion and give the game away…).

Having been on the road for five hours or so, we were reaching cabin fever point, so we parked up in a layby advertising a trail to a viewpoint and had another of what was now becoming our customary rock-face scrambles. 20 minutes later, and we were atop the hill in the sunshine with a panoramic view of the park with its mountains, valleys and cascading waterfalls, and we were all alone – just blissful. We chilled for a good while until the rumbles of thunder got too loud to ignore anymore (we were, after all, the highest and pointiest things in the immediate area), and so we headed back to the car and made our way to our hotel – Wuksachi Lodge.

As we were now in the land of the Giant Sequoias, I should fill you in on some of the key facts about these remarkable trees.

1. They only grow naturally in a narrow 260-mile strip on the western slopes of the Sierra Nevada mountains, primarily at an elevation of between 5,000 and 7,000 feet – this is because that altitude offers the best levels of humidity, rainfall, sunlight etc.
2. With a lifespan of up to 3,000 years, they are the world's third longest living tree species, can grow as high as 300 feet, with branches up to eight feet in diameter and bark up to two feet thick (which also is flame-resistant and therefore gives them the same level of protection from fire as the Giant Redwoods). Although most of the tallest get struck by lightning, causing the top 30% of the tree to fall off; this, though, does not kill them and they continue to grow outwards rather than upwards, putting on the beef rather than the height, as it were…

3. They were extensively logged during the 19th century, before we understood the damage we were doing – an astonishing 95% of the trees were felled – however, rather sadly, the resulting wood is brittle and therefore not a great deal of use to us. Doh!
4. The largest Giant Sequoia is the General Sherman and it is the largest living organism in the world – please don't anyone start on me about The Great Barrier Reef – because although at only 83m (275 feet) tall, the diameter and circumference of its base are 11m (36 feet) and 31m (102 feet) respectively. This gives it a total mass of 1,487 cubic metres (52,500 cubic feet) – which is the equivalent of just over 13 double decker buses. Now, put that in your pipe and smoke it, Lothian Transport...

38. Trees That Please, Part II
9th June 2019

We woke early with dawn already broken, the day looked good as we had a bright blue sky and the sun was sporting rather a dashing hat. We were up and out quickly as we wanted to get into the woods before too many other folk were about, as the peace and tranquillity is best experienced when you're on your own – and also, there's a much greater chance of seeing bears…

There are 40 officially listed groves of Giant Sequoias in the whole park, with the number of trees in each one ranging from about 20 to several thousand. The most easily accessible grove is Giant Forest, which the park road winds through and so it was there that we headed. We parked in a layby and walked into Long Meadow, a very pretty watery glade, which acts as a sponge, retaining moisture from the mountain snowmelt and releasing it slowly during the year, ensuring that there is always water for the forest.

We followed the path which winds around the perimeter of the meadow and is called Big Tree Trail, this took us amongst more than 100 trees in the grove. We spent an hour and half wandering along and off the trail and it was wonderfully quiet and still; we came across deer and groundhogs who were about their daily business of feeding, playing, etc. before the crowds appeared – the beauty, peace and stillness really cannot be understated enough.

We headed back to the hotel for some breakfast and then were out again by 10, when we made first for one of the park's main attractions, the General Sherman tree, which as previously described is the park's (and world's) largest. At 2,100 years old, it is something of a middle-ager, as it's only two-thirds of the way through its 3,000-year likely lifespan; so unless something should befall it, it is going to retain its title for some time to come. Light-hearted comments aside, it is a majestic tree, 103 feet around at the base and so tall, with so much upper branch growth, it is very hard to see the top, a true wonder.

We then struck off along the two-mile Congress Trail, so called because it winds past The Senate and House Groves as well as the President Tree (which is the third largest in the park). The path also took us quite literally through a tree, as they have cut a tunnel in one which fell onto the path several decades ago. Due to the density of their wood and depending on where they fall, it can take several hundred years for a mature Sequoia to rot, thus providing both a long-term food source for the bears (they eat ants and termites which burrow in rotting trees), as well as a slow-release of nutrients back into the environment.

Having completed the Congress Trail, we took another couple of paths, which wound through further groves, up and down hillsides and over streams, before ending up at the Grant

Museum which has displays, exhibits and information about the trees, as well as the history of the park and plans for its future care. Fortunately, this does appear to be well in hand, which wasn't always the case as I had previously read that in the 1965, the National Park Service struck a deal with Walt Disney which would have allowed him to build a Disneyland Ski Resort in the middle of the park. I can't think of many things more damaging to this sort of environment than building a theme park, can you? Once word got out, the decision was challenged in court, but it dragged on for years and years and it was not until 1978 when Jimmy Carter signed the National Parks and Recreation Act that the scheme was finally shelved. I find that utterly incredible.

Anyhow, digression about the House of Mouse and its suspect plans aside, we then took one of the park shuttle buses back up to the car park for our picnic and a sit down. I should add that the National Park Service runs a number of free bus services along the roads as it helps reduce congestion as well as pollution and makes it a much more accessible place for all.

Lunch done and dusted, we agreed that one more hike was in order, so we drove round to the trails which encircle Crescent and Log Meadows. Both are similar to the Long Meadow we had walked around in the morning, but they have a couple of interesting trees which were worth seeing. First up was Chimney Tree, whose trunk has been hollowed out by fire, enabling you to stand inside and see all the way up, about 60 feet to the sky, presenting really quite a unique view – and whilst it may be burnt out, it still lives.

The second was Tharp's Log, which is also a hollowed-out tree, but lies on its side, having fallen a couple of hundred years ago, and was big enough to be used as a shelter by early pioneers coming through the forest. Its name comes from Hale Tharp, who is reputedly the first Non-Native American to go into the Giant Forest. It was still possible to go into the tree and see the tables, shelves and beds which were used by those pioneers, and when we poked our heads inside, we found a groundhog who was too busy gnawing away at the inside of the trunk to notice us, which is just as it should be, don't you think?

39. The Golden City, Part I
12th June 2019

With our time at Sequoia at an end, we checked out of Wuksachi Lodge early on and made our way out of the park and just on the off chance that we might spot a bear or two we took our time and made frequent stops along the road. Although we saw more groundhogs, elk and many birds of prey unfortunately, this didn't happen, which meant our visit was bearless, but that wasn't too disappointing, as it does mean that they continue to live peacefully and undisturbed in the forests, and also they retain their status as the best hiders in the forest. Perhaps we should have brought honey…

Returning via the roads we had taken to enter the park, we made our way to Interstate 5, which traverses the state (and indeed the country) from top to bottom (all the way from Mexico up to Canada). This particular section runs for approximately 150 miles, along the bottom of the baking hot San Joaquin valley – known locally as the Central Valley –

which is blessed with having some of the most fertile land in the country and is where 60% of the fruit and veg sold in the US is grown. This is despite both the multi-year drought they have been experiencing and the intense heat they have – according to the car thermometer, the mercury didn't drop below 32 Celsius while we were there driving through the valley.

Aside from the fertile soil, the main reason it is so productive is in large part thanks to the California aqueduct system, which also runs the length of the state and down the valley, delivering millions of gallons of water every day to the people who live in the parched south of the state and also used to irrigate the 750,000 acres of farmland.

Turning west and leaving the valley behind, we drove up and over the mountains which form its western flank and descended towards the cities which make up the San Francisco metropolitan area. Having spent much of the previous fortnight in remote locations and on quiet roads, it was a little bit unnerving at first, to suddenly find ourselves in the midst of heavy urban traffic. Fortunately, the lately dormant urban warrior in me soon reasserted himself and we soon found ourselves being swept along by the freeway tide with everyone else.

We entered the city via the very impressive five miles long San Mateo bridge, which is roughly halfway down San Francisco Bay and having found our way to the Airbnb apartment in the College Hill area of the city, we decided that as it was getting late, we should quit while we were ahead and just chill for the evening.

San Francisco is famed for its fog and so the next morning, we were pleasantly surprised to find the city bathed in warm sunshine with clear blue skies and barely a breath of wind. As far as we were concerned there was only one thing for us – a good walk. Our first stop was a visit to a TV and film set and prop making business on the southern edge of the city and once done, we drove down to the Embarcadero, where the harbour was built. There are still 40 or so of the old quays where ships carrying goods from all around the world used to dock to load and unload cargo. Sadly, with the exception of those used by cruise liners and the tourist and commuter ferries, none of the quays operate for ships these days, as all the merchant shipping now docks at the relatively recently built Port of San Francisco which is further around the Bay. For the rest of the quays, many of the buildings have been converted for other commercial uses, such as museums, restaurants, shops and car parks – which whilst not necessarily ideal is certainly better than being torn down.

Strolling on, we saw the now decommissioned Alcatraz prison all on its lonesome perched on its island in the middle of the bay, looking stark, gloomy and every inch the grimmest prison in the country it was reputed to be. We watched the sealions at Pier 39, basking in the sun, pushing and shoving each other about and barking noisily at everyone and no one. They've been in residence at this spot since 1989 and prior to that, their 'home base' was one of the islands underneath the Oakland Bridge, however on the 15th of October of that year, they all suddenly left and started arriving at Pier 39. Two days later came the major earthquake which caused a section of the Oakland Bridge to collapse, so the legend now has it that if the sealions leave the harbour, an earthquake is potentially on the cards…For those seismically minded, they were still there when we left, and according to seal-cam, they are there today as well.

Walking on further down the quayside, we made a stop at the Boudin Bakery at Fisherman's Wharf. This was founded in 1849 by French immigrants and is famed for its sourdough bread, which back in the days of the gold rush was very popular with prospectors because it stayed fresh for a lot longer than regular bread. It was there that we paused for lunch and had their signature dish – fish chowder served inside a sourdough boule, it was both very tasty and very filling – this is a place I thoroughly recommend.

Our next stop was the Ghirardelli chocolate factory, which is another San Francisco institution. Unfortunately, they no longer make chocolate on site – they moved production to a modern facility several years ago – but there is a factory shop still in the complex where they hand out free samples to anyone visiting the store, therefore automatically qualifying it for extra tourist brownie points in my book.

To finish our day, what better way than to grab a ride on one of the cable cars which make their very stately progress up and over the hilly streets of the city. With my little bit of local knowledge, I knew that if we walked up the route of one of the lines for a couple of stops, we would be able to ride for free, as passengers are only charged if they board at the beginning of the line. I expect this is less to do with giving freeloaders a happy day and more because the driver is concerned with keeping his car on the cable and braking at the appropriate moments. Thus, as it approached, we stepped out, waved to the driver and boarded, riding it all the way to Union Square, with us stood on the side runners and hanging on, hair blowing in the wind – it felt very, very cool.

40. The Golden City, Part II
14th June 2019

For our second full day in the city, we wanted to go and see the Golden Gate Bridge, but rather than drive over, we wanted to do it up close and what better way to do this than by bike. As with most cities these days there are a great many places which hire out bikes in the city and as they're all roughly the same price, we picked a firm based in the Haight-Ashbury area of the city, as it was just a quick cab ride away from where we were staying and we also wanted to check it out.

In the '60s, Haight-Ashbury was the epicentre of the flower power and counterculture movement in the US, and once this died down, the area evolved during the '70s to become one of the first acknowledged and recognised gay and lesbian quarters of any US city. A great many reminders of its key roles in the development of modern societal social attitudes remain to this day and can best be seen in the psychedelic murals and messages of peace, love and harmony as well as the relaxed atmosphere and warm welcome from the residents and shop owners.

We chose electric bikes again, as having driven the streets the day before, we knew that there were some really punishing hills to tackle, and as we wanted to see as much as possible, it made sense to give ourselves some extra power. Our route took us along the edges of Golden Gate Park and then down to the Presidio, which until the late '80s was a US Army base, but following the end of the Cold War, it was decommissioned, and its ownership passed to the National Park Service, who now manage it as an urban parkland and it's a real treat with its sweeping views of San Francisco bay, the bridges and the city.

Once we had arrived at the bridge, we paused at the gift shop which had all the standard touristy nick-nacks all with pictures of the structure emblazoned on them – tea towels, mugs, caps, jigsaws etc.; but amongst all this there was one item in particular which caught our eyes and was a genuine contender for purchase. In tribute to their local climate, instead of snow-globes, they sell a fog-globe of the bridge, which, when shaken, clouds billow around the bridge enveloping it in a blanket of impenetrable fug which then slowly clears. Genius! We were sorely tempted...

However, our reason for being there was not to peruse the gift shop, we were there for the bridge and so with our eyes and senses having reached maximum-tat-capacity, we pedalled away and onto the bridge. It was quite slow going to start with, as in addition to the many pedestrians who were making their way along, the wind was gusting to 50 mph and seemed to be coming at us from every direction. This made steering and speed control a tad tricky, as just when we thought we would never get moving, a gust from behind would shove us briskly along, before a side blow would buffet us expletively close to the railing and a potential free-fall entry to the bay with resulting consequences at best the loss of the deposit on the bike. Once on and into the middle, though, it was worth all the effort, as the views towards the city and over the bay were superb – it was such a clear day, we could see all the way to the mountains, which until recently we had been in, as well as panoramic vista of the harbour and city waterfront.

On the other side, we went into the pretty old fishing village of Sausalito, where we sat on the sea wall and had our picnic while we watched the sealions and herons vying with each other to catch fish. Lunch done, we cycled around the village and then back over the bridge and down to the promenade, which leads all the way back to Fisherman's Wharf. Here, we paused for ice cream and to watch some of the very brave souls who were swimming in Aquatic Park, which is a specially sectioned off part of the harbour ('sectioned' here seems a very appropriate word...). From there though, it was all uphill back to Haight-Ashbury, but, as we had plenty of battery power left, it was plain sailing for us on the bikes and we covered the five up and down miles in 20 not at all exhausting minutes. I should also say that San Francisco is an excellent city for cycling, as it is very well served for bike paths and dedicated bike lanes, which make the negotiation of traffic a great deal easier than in most places and these together with its blend of 19th and early 20th century building gives it a much more European feel.

The following day was our last, so after tidying up and checking out, we headed to another SF highlight, Lombard Street, which, with a gradient of 31.5%, is by far the steepest street in the city and reputedly the steepest residential street in America. Very sensibly, given the 2,500 tourist vehicles which drive down it every day, it's a downhill one-way street, the direction being downwards, but even so, extreme caution and a good set of brake pads are essential, as every one of the eight hairpin bends is tight and hair-raising.

We finished our day with Sourdough Boule Chowder from Boudin at the waterfront again and a really cracking mint choc chip from the Baked Bear Ice Cream and Cookie shop. Only the brave (and very hungry) go for the ice cream cookie sandwich, which features four vast scoops of your flavour choice, stuck between two 20cm cookies – bring your fat pants.

41. Journey's End
16th June 2019

Having finished our ice creams at Fisherman's Wharf, Evie and I made our way to San Francisco airport and the mood was unsurprisingly a little blue. We talked through all our highlights and tried to keep cheerful, but we knew what was coming. This was the end and we weren't looking forward to it.

Evie got checked in for her flight which was to take her to her next adventure – she was off to build treehouses in India (how cool is that?) – whereas mine was a little less exotic. I walked back to the car park and got into the Jeep and had a little cry as all the adventures and excitement we had had were over. This didn't last too long as I still had a 500-mile drive south to San Diego, which is where my flight was departing from, in two days' time. I put some music on and tried to sing along, but the mood wasn't with it, so instead, I listened to an audio book we'd started a few days earlier called Barbarian Days. This, for me, is hands down the best book about surfing and the surfing experience ever written; it is by William Finnegan, who's long been a writer for the New Yorker and it tells his story going back to the late '60s of how he started surfing, his motivations, how it developed and morphed over the years to his current relationship with it. It is less a story about surfing and more one about life. I highly recommend it.

I paused overnight at a motel just off the interstate, before heading off again early the following morning. I got down to and around the LA freeways without too much trouble and drove on to San Clemente, where I had arranged to meet Donna for a farewell lunch at Sonny's on the main street. This was a fitting end to my trip as we had become good friends during my stay and so having a final meal with her was perfect way to say goodbye to the town I had come to regard as my home from home.

Monument Valley from the plane

Having finished our meal, we said our farewells and I headed on down the coast to San Diego, I stopped at a charity shop and gave away a number of things I could not get into my luggage. These included a SodaStream, a couple of boogie boards and my skateboard, which, as much as I would have liked to have brought home, it was just too big for my case – and at least this way, I reckoned it would go to another home, where it would be cherished.

Grand Canyon from the plane

I passed a quiet night in a motel near the airport and this was followed by an early start for my homeward journey. My flight was San Diego to Edinburgh via Philadelphia, which might sound a bit of a pain, but it did mean me not having to travel through Heathrow, which, I think is one of the world's worst airports – too crowded, too noisy and too unfriendly. For me, once through security, I much prefer to find the right gate and chill, rather than be herded along overcrowded winding pathways, hemmed in by shops, restaurants and bars. It often feels as though commercial greed is prioritised far above customer comfort – I understand the need to generate revenue and profit, but does it always have to done in such a cold, calculating and impolite way?

The Rockies from the plane

Arriving in Philly, I had nine hours to kill, however I had planned ahead and a few weeks before this, I had contacted my cousin Patrick, who lives just outside the city and so on arrival, I walked off the plane, out of the terminal building and met up with him for a final dose of tourist sightseeing. He showed me around the centre of town – Independence Hall, the Liberty Bell, old town, etc. as well as having a walk on the lovely riverside path with its street food vendors, bars and other recently created attractions. He then took me to an excellent city centre bar, which had around 30 or so ales on sale as well as some great food. As it had been a few years since we had last met, we sat and chatted for a good few hours, swapping all our various news and asking after respective family and also agreeing that we were both flummoxed by the continuing appeal of Donald Trump. It was the perfect way to finish off my odyssey…

Independence Hall, Philly

42. Epilogue – Keeping It Real
17th June 2019

So, the trip had ended and I was back home in Aberdour. Over the course of the 18 days on the road trip, Evie and I clocked up 3,363 miles and spent 83.5 hours driving – that's nearly three and a half days – and every one of those hours and miles was a joy. What fun we had!

My time in San Clemente was equally good, and I worked out that I had managed to surf on 45 of the 58 days I was there, and what a joy it was that Alex, Harriet and Jenny were all also able to come out and join in the fun. The work for the food bank and helping at the adaptive surfer sessions added extra depth, vitality and some personal connection to the area. I made some new friends, and to top it all, I even came back with a suntan – me, Blackpool Boy! Who would have thought it…

Prior to coming on this trip, I had never kept a diary or made any written record of events and happenings in my life, but I really enjoyed doing it as I found it therapeutic, entertaining and helped me get my head around the fact that I had the chance to do this amazing thing and it has helped keep the memories fresh and alive.

Now, as a final sign-off.

When you're on the road, it's good to mix things up a little and have a bit of fun along the way as things could easily get a bit boring and stale and so Evie suggested that when we ask people to take photos of us, rather than the usual strike a pose and click, why don't we jump in the air and get them to capture that instead – Jump Shots, channelling our inner Van Halen, as it were.

So, we did. It rarely worked first time (heads or feet were often missing from pictures, other times we would already have landed, etc.) and so several attempts were required before we could be captured in mid-flight. But it never failed to bring a smile to people's faces – the results are below. See if you can look at them without laughing, I know I can't...

San Luis Obispo

Big Sur

Golden Gate Bridge

Lost Coast

Crater Lake

Lake Tahoe

Sequoia National Park